For anyone wishing to create financial security through real estate investing, *Cash Flow Forever!* is one of the best books I have ever read. It is full of "ground up" life stories that are easily understood and enthusiastically written. A must read!
— Charlie Bartlett, CCIM Hawkins Edwards

With his book, *Cash Flow Forever!* Jeff puts his expertise into digestible information helpful to anyone looking to go into the field of real estate investing.
— Linn Parish Deputy Editor, Spokane Journal of Business

Cash Flow Forever! is an honest look at investing and holding real estate to create generations of wealth. You will find this easy to read book hard to put down and will wonder why you didn't start creating "Cash Flow Forever" at an earlier age.
— Dave Black SIOR CCIM CEO, NAI Black

This book provides a unique perspective on real estate investing. The author sheds light on new concepts that most real estate investment books skip over.
— John Sinclair, Broker, Keller Williams Realty

Jeff Johnson generously shares a lifetime of knowledge in real estate investing. Anyone who dares to invest should read this book.
— Chris Kopczynski, President, Kop Construction, Inc.

A great book for those looking to learn the basics of real estate investing. Jeff shares with the reader his years of experience investing in retail, office, industrial and multifamily real estate.
— Barclay Klingel, CEO, Cyrus O'Leary's Pies

Cash Flow Forever! is both a great primer for those just beginning in real estate investing and a "real world reference book" for those with experience.

—Gerald Smith, D.D.S., M.S.D., ABO

Jeff Johnson shares many important financial concepts required to be a successful real estate investor. His insights on financial capacity, diversification and the accumulation of assets are invaluable.

—Jeff McCloskey, President, McCloskey Construction

This book provides detailed instruction on real estate investing in a format that is easy for anyone to understand. Once I started to read the book I couldn't put it down until I was finished!

—Frank Takes, Takes Family, L.P

Cash Flow Forever!

Cash Flow Forever!

The Real Secrets of
Real Estate Investing

Jeff K. Johnson
CCIM SIOR

View Point Publishing, LLC
130 West High Drive
Spokane, WA 99203

Cash Flow Forever!: The Real Secrets of Real Estate Investing

Printed in the United States of America

ISBN: 978-1-4895-2448-5

Disclaimer

Real estate investing is a risky business. The ideas, recommendations, and opinions provided in this book are based on the author's experience and research and are not infallible. The author is not providing legal advice or any guarantee that these ideas will work for the reader. The reader must put these ideas and concepts into practice at their own risk. The reader should seek legal advice and professional assistance before acting on any information in this book. Laws and events change over time and those laws and events may no longer have the same effect or application as they did when this book was written. No information in this book is or shall be construed as an offer or solicitation for the purchase or sale of any property or security.

Dedications & Acknowledgments

I must dedicate this book to my loving wife Kae, who has stuck with me through the thick and thin that comes with getting started in real estate investing—especially when I borrowed more money than I should have or sold the family boat to purchase yet another building. She has listened to me say for years, "Honey, we are almost there." So thanks for sticking with me, Kae. And yes, we are almost there!

I also need to thank my parents, Ken and Carol Johnson, for raising me in a loving home and preparing me very well for life. From my mother I learned hard work, creativity and the pursuit of adventure. From my father I learned a love for people, a love of the outdoors and problem solving skills.

Then there are the many wonderful mentors who have guided me along the path of life with encouragement, education and friendship. I have had so many mentors that I do not have room to acknowledge all of them here; if I tried to do so I would be concerned about leaving someone out. So, thank you to the many mentors I have had over the years!

I must specifically thank two of my real estate mentors who have had the most impact on my life. Frank Takes was my first real estate mentor. I met Frank when I was working as a church janitor in Cedar Rapids, Iowa. Frank gave me a copy of the book *Think and Grow Rich* by

Napoleon Hill, which I have read from cover to cover many times, and still keep handy on my bookshelf for quick reference. Then, he sent me across the street to the Town and Country Shopping Center to purchase a 19-cent spiral notebook in which he instructed me to write out goals for my life. From Frank I learned the foundations of goal setting and real estate investing.

In 1985, I met Ron McCloskey who educated me in the finer points of money management, and real estate investing and development. Ron is a great teacher, partner, and friend to this day.

Thank you, Frank and Ron.

Also, many thanks to my editor and literary consultant, Linn Parish. Linn you did a great job of organizing and cleaning up my patchwork of ideas. With your guidance and literary skills the first draft of this book came together nicely.

This book would not be finished without the tireless efforts of Lori Schlect. Lori helped me improve and expand the original draft. Then she worked diligently to proof and polish the final version of the book. Thanks Lori! We finished!

And I must thank Russ Davis of Grey Dog Press. Russ thanks for your patience and encouragement. Thanks for helping me reach my goal of getting this book published. Your industry knowledge and skills were invaluable.

And finally a big thanks to the many friends and clients who have guided and encouraged me as I have worked to learn and develop my real estate investing and career skills. Thank you!

Foreword

Thank you for investing in this book and in yourself. I hope that you will find the stories and information that I share in this book to be educational, entertaining and motivating. I also hope that the key concepts that are revealed here will give you valuable ideas that you can use to build your personal net worth through real estate investing.

I have been gathering and refining the concepts shared in this book for many years. I have read about these concepts in books, learned them from my many mentors and practiced them myself many times over. These concepts are easier to put into writing than they are to put into action. Putting them into action will take hard work and maybe a change in your thinking patterns. But you can do it!

I have been very blessed with the path that life has taken me. I will admit that I am a very goal oriented person and I have charted much of my life's course by continually setting new and larger goals. Fortunately, the goals I set over the years have intersected with many wonderful opportunities that came my way. And many of those came from the great people I have met and have had the pleasure of working with. Even considering the normal challenges of life, I have been very fortunate. As my friend Bruce Ellwein says, "...*and then life comes along.*" Life does come along, and it presents us with numerous challenges as we work to achieve our goals, but by persevering through them, we gain much satisfaction as we look back and see what we have come through and accomplished.

My main goal in writing this book is to share with you how you can experience many of the same successes that I have been fortunate to achieve in my real estate investing.

Real estate investing is like life. Half of the battle in life is finding the right path. The other half of the battle is working to stay on the path and continuing to make forward progress, no matter how difficult the obstacles become. So please follow along as I work to lay out a well defined path for real estate investing.

At heart, I am just your average small town Iowa boy. I was blessed to have loving parents who taught me about faith, hard work and serving others. One of the benefits of growing up in Iowa is that you learn how to work hard at a very young age. This becomes a pattern for life and a very important life skill. You learn how to keep pressing onward no matter how hard the challenges are, or no matter how worn down you become in the daily battle.

As I mentioned in the Dedications and Acknowledge-ments section, I was blessed to have many amazing mentors to guide me and give me encouragement. In addition to having great mentors, it helps to have creative vision, which you may find to be both a blessing and a challenge. Having a lot of ideas is exciting, but can send you in too many directions at once!. I believe we can all develop creative vision as we learn from others. Successful entrepreneurs are the ones who take their creative ideas and actually turn them into something. They act on their vision and ideas. They have the ability to focus on what is really important and to push the less important things aside.

I hope this book will give you a fresh vision and direction as it relates to your financial goals and your interest in real estate investing. This is a book of concepts. All the lessons and key concepts of real estate investing that I have learned are spelled out in this book. If you can grasp and put them into practice, over time you will develop your own pattern of successful real estate investing. Most of these lessons and concepts are very simple to define but it will take a lot of determination and discipline to put them into action.

I wish you the very best as you work to achieve your real estate investing goals.

Contents

*Activity makes more men's
fortunes than cautiousness.*
Marquis De Vauvenargues

*Improvement of one's economic position is helped
more by cool persistence than by hot enthusiasm.*
William Feather

~ 1 ~
How I Got Started

"Cash Flow Forever: The Real Secrets of Real Estate Investing!" The title of this book is not meant to project the idea that real estate investing is easy or that it is by any means a way to get rich quickly. On the contrary, it reflects the idea that with hard work and by following tried and true real estate investing principles, real estate is a wonderful vehicle to create wealth and develop long term cash flow. In this book I look forward to sharing with you what I have learned about real estate investing over the last thirty seven years. I have enjoyed a wonderful career in the real estate business and it has been very personally rewarding. The friends I have made and the satisfaction of accomplishment I have enjoyed are far greater than the monetary gains I have been fortunate to achieve. Let's begin.

When my wife and I were first married, we lived in a small apartment in Cedar Rapids, Iowa. We had both dropped out of college not exactly knowing what we wanted to do for careers. I was working as a church janitor, and my wife had a job as a customer service representative at the local utility, Iowa Illinois Gas and Electric Company. Our rent was $125 per month, but we barely made enough money to make ends meet. Things were so tight that for a few months, we lived off of bread, water and tomatoes from a small garden our landlord let us plant in the backyard. Some nights, my wife would be crying when she came home from work, because she didn't know how we would pay the rent or other bills for that matter.

I wanted to be a good husband and provide for my new wife, so I began searching for ways to make more money. In an attempt to improve our desperate situation, I decided to try selling residential real estate to augment the income from my job as a church janitor.

Though my real estate career didn't produce a flood of new income right away, I started to learn about something I'd known little about previously: money. Having grown up in an average, middle-class family in a small Iowa farm town, I had wonderful, loving parents, but wealth accumulation wasn't part of our everyday world.

In the early days of my real estate career, I was fascinated by the success of the seasoned salespeople in my company and I was determined to learn from them. I also developed a desire to be financially successful and decided to learn everything I could about money and investing. I began to read every book I could on the subject and sought counsel from anyone who was willing to share their secrets of success with me.

Over the years, I learned from many successful individuals about investing and managing money. Real estate investing in particular was a key component of what I learned. I was able to witness firsthand the step-by-step process through which these individuals made millions of dollars investing in real estate. As I watched, I began to formulate my own plans to achieve financial success in the real estate industry. I applied the principles you'll read about in this book, and over the years I have been blessed with financial success beyond my wildest dreams.

One of the first real estate investors I met was a man by the name of Cliff Doe. If we had cell phones in Iowa back in 1975, I might not have gotten my first lesson in real estate investing at such a young age. Thankfully, it wasn't as easy to get a hold of someone back then, and a simple series of events led me down what proved to be a lucrative path. Let me explain.

I was just getting started at my new job at John Zachar Realtors, and I wrote an offer on a house that was listed for sale by a well-established broker named Cliff Doe. Cliff owned his own company, and his for-sale signs included an illustration of a deer—deer, Doe, you see the connection—but the deer looked more like a donkey. The signs always amused me. Having never met Cliff before, I was curious to find out what he was like—and eager to hand him the offer I had written up.

I called Cliff's office only to be told he was doing some work on a house that didn't have a phone. His assistant gave me the address, and I drove out to see him.

The neighborhood was filled with gorgeous, high-end homes, some of which were still under construction. Cliff, however, wasn't in one of the luxurious new homes. He was in an old farmhouse in the field right next door to the development.

I entered the old farmhouse to find Cliff stripping wallpaper. It didn't make sense to me; why would a successful broker be working so hard on an old house? A better plan, it seemed to me, would be to bulldoze the old home and build a nice, new one like those a stone's throw away.

But Cliff had plans which he was kind enough to share with me when I asked what he was doing. The farmhouse was situated on three acres of land that he was planning to subdivide into three lots. He would renovate the farmhouse extensively so that it fit in with the rest of the neighborhood, and he and his wife would move in. Then, he would sell the two empty lots and make enough money to pay for the newly renovated farmhouse and the land it sat on. Wow, a little ingenuity and some hard work resulted in a free and clear home!

As it turned out, this was the 22nd project like this he and his wife had undertaken. They had made a career out of buying houses, moving in, and fixing them up while they lived there—then selling them when they were ready.

Suddenly, the offer I was so eager to present took a back seat to this new concept; it was my first glimpse into the moneymaking opportunities in real estate. I asked question after question before finally doing the business I set out to do, giving him the offer. The experience was so profound I can't even remember whether the offer was accepted!

Around the same time, I began to get to know the man I consider to be my first mentor. Frank Takes was one of the few commercial real estate salespeople in the 35-agent office where I worked. At 37 years old, he hadn't been in real estate long, and his plan was to get out of day to day sales quickly. He wanted to buy, fix up and rent out homes to generate income—and reach some financial goals he set for himself. Shortly after I met Frank, he left

John Zachar Realtors to focus on this venture.

As Frank got started in his search for homes and small apartment buildings, he kindly enlisted my help in finding properties, even though he was capable of doing so himself. He was looking for run-down houses in need of repair or distressed properties that needed to be sold due to divorce or bankruptcy. Each week, I'd scan the new listings for Frank, and I quickly learned how to be an expert real estate bargain hunter. For one stretch of time, I was selling Frank about one home a week. The entire time, I asked a lot of questions and observed carefully.

Being only 20 years old and not overly assertive or confident, I wasn't entirely comfortable with the idea of borrowing money and dealing with tenants. Following Frank's lead, though, I set some of my own financial goals and got up the courage to make my first offer on a home. The woman who owned it was selling it herself. She wanted $16,800 and would carry the contract herself for $1,000 down. I made what I thought was a low-ball offer of $16,000 with $500 down, and she accepted it. Shocked, I quickly got cold feet, in part because I simply panicked, but largely because I didn't have the cash for the $500 down payment. Frank took the deal off my hands and bought the house instead. He fixed it up and sold it soon thereafter for $20,000.

A short time later, I mustered the courage to buy a small, two-bedroom home for $20,000 with $2,000 down. I didn't have $500 before, and I certainly didn't have $2,000 when I made the second offer. Regardless, I was determined. One of the sales associates in my office offered to lend me $1,000, and together with my real estate commission, I cobbled together the balance.

My wife and I moved out of our apartment and into our first house, knowing we wouldn't be there long. The house needed a relatively small amount of work. We cleaned the junk out of the garage, took some debris out of the yard, and trimmed up the lawn and bushes. I built a small patio in the backyard and a planter box near the front steps, then painted the outside and wallpapered the inside of the house.

Only three months after we bought it, the house was spotless and ready to sell. We put the house on the market for $23,900 and sold it within a month for just below the asking price. After paying half a commission and some closing costs I made my first big money in real estate: $2,837.

Now, this might not seem like a lot of money, especially when you consider the hassle of moving in and out of a home in a matter of months. But in 1975, it was a decent amount of money for a guy who was just getting started. I couldn't wait to do it again, and set out to find a more challenging fixer upper.

After a few weeks of searching, I found a two-bedroom home in a nice neighborhood listed at $21,500. A widow who lived 35 miles away had been renting the house out for a number of years, but she decided she was too old to deal with it any more. The house had been on the market for a while, and she wanted badly to unload it.

The house was in rough shape. The roof was failing, and the eaves had rotted out. Birds had been nesting in a large, unfinished second-floor attic. I took some friends to see the house one night, and when we turned on the basement light, we watched in horror as dozens of cockroaches ran for cover.

I initially offered $18,500 with $2,000 down, but after some negotiation, we agreed to a $19,000 sale price and $2,500 down. I had enough money to cover the down payment from the sale of the first home but not enough money to fix it up. I estimated it would cost $6,000 to do all of the needed repairs and decided to borrow the money.

But who would lend money to a now-21-year-old kid who was still wet behind the ears? I inquired at a number of banks and was repeatedly turned down. Eventually, I went to a banker who was friends with a co-worker. The co-worker reported I was hard working and dependable, and the banker decided to take a chance on me.

With the money in hand for the needed repairs, I busted my backside for six months, working hard on evenings and weekends to get the house in tip-top shape. I converted the unfinished attic into a large master bedroom by adding a dormer, which turned the sloped rear ceiling of the attic into an open room with two windows. This change added a lot of value to the project. When all was said and done, I listed the now-immaculate home at $37,950, and in a strong real estate market, I sold it for $450 below asking price. I made $9,250 on that house.

It was 1977. I was 22 years old, and I now had $11,750 in my pocket. Even now, that's a good chunk of change, and it was a bigger chunk then.

My wife and I repeated the fix-up-and-sell process two more times and made more money on each home than we had on the prior transactions. We didn't call it house flipping back then—and this isn't a book about house flipping—but what we were doing was a version of this business model that made a lot of people money prior to our current recession. A lot of those folks lost big when the market took a turn for the worse, and the principles I will introduce will work whether the market is going up or down. Believe me, I've done this in good economic times and in bad.

This is still a great way to obtain seed capital for beginning your real estate investing career if you are young and have a flexible schedule. It can work at any stage in life, but can be challenging if you have to carry out your normal life activities in the midst of a remodeling mess. If your improvements are limited to redecorating, it is not so bad. If you fixed up one home over a period of a year or so like we did, it makes it easier to live through.

After starting with the fixer upper homes, I moved up to small apartment buildings that needed upgrading and repairs. From there I advanced to land, office buildings, retail buildings and other types of real estate investment properties.

As I learned, I kept notes of what worked—and what didn't work—so someday I could share those thoughts with others. In this book, I will share with you one of the greatest real estate investment concepts I have ever learned. I will show you how to enjoy incredible cash flow from your real estate investments. I have read dozens of books on real estate investing, and none of them include this concept. It is a contrarian concept used only by a few investors I have met who are very private about their investments and their money.

I will share with you a proven way to generate cash to start your real estate investing career regardless of your current financial situation, and I will reveal the pitfalls of the much-publicized "get rich quick with nothing down" programs you see in some books and on cable television. I will also show you how to find real estate bargains that can instantly grow your net worth.

What I'm about to share with you could change your life. You can begin now to build a real estate *Cash Flow Forever* that will support you for the rest of your life. It will put your children through college, make the payments on a vacation home, and allow you to travel the world. You just have to follow these easy-to-understand steps. Come on! Let's get started!

What's hard makes us great.
Tom Hanks

~ Notes ~

~ 2 ~
The Greatest Real Estate
Secret Never Told

After getting started with my real estate career in Iowa, my wife and I moved to Spokane, Washington, with the goal of living in a larger city with good access to outdoor activities. Shortly after moving to Spokane, we became friends with a couple named Steve and Judy. I didn't know it at the time, but they would share with me the greatest real estate secret never told.

Steve and Judy were interested in achieving financial independence through real estate investing, and my wife and I enjoyed talking with them about money and investing. During one of our discussions, they told us about the first rental property they had acquired about seven years earlier. The property consisted of two homes on one lot: a larger three-bedroom house toward the front and a small one-bedroom home at the back.

Both houses were in a state of disrepair when they purchased the property, and they spent a considerable amount of time and money fixing them up. After they fixed up the two homes, they rented them out. The large home was rented for $300 per month and the small one was rented for $175 per month. So their gross income from the two homes totaled $475 per month.

What they told me next shocked me. They had already paid off the mortgage on this property. I asked them how they had managed to accomplish this. They said that they collected the rent from their tenants, paid the operating expenses, paid the mortgage and had cash flow left over. Then they had taken their cash flow and made extra payments on the mortgage rather than reinvest or spend that money. I was amazed that making extra principal payments on a mortgage could pay it off so quickly. I had never heard of this concept before.

I couldn't believe it. At the time, I couldn't imagine owning property that was paid for, and here my friends were, collecting $5,700 in income annually from this one property. This was my first hint at the greatest secret about real estate investing. If you buy real estate, keep it rented, and work hard to pay off the mortgage, you will have *Cash Flow Forever!*

A few years later, I was doing some work for a successful local builder and developer who told me he wouldn't take on a project unless the income was sufficient to pay off the mortgage in 10 years. Pay off a large commercial property mortgage in 10 years? *No way,* I thought. *Maybe you could do that with a small inexpensive rental house but not with a commercial mortgage. He must be blowing smoke.*

Shortly thereafter, I asked a real estate investor I knew named Dick if it was really possible to pay off properties that quickly. He told me about two buildings he had paid off—a fast-food restaurant building that housed a Mexican restaurant and a large retail building rented by a furniture store. The restaurant building brought in $3,500 a month, and the furniture store cut him a rent check for $10,000 every month. Once again, I was totally flabbergasted. Dick and his wife were receiving $162,000 a year from just two buildings. These two paid-for buildings were providing Dick and his wife an amazing income which would continue for the rest of their lives. *Cash Flow Forever!*

Now my former ideas about real estate investing took on a totally new direction. For the first time, I began to realize that it was possible to invest in real estate, pay off the mortgages and have *Cash Flow Forever*—so long as you take good care of your properties and keep them rented. I have read a lot of books on real estate investing, but I have yet to read a book that promotes this investment philosophy. The vast majority of the books I have read all focus on borrowing as much money as you can, putting down the smallest down payment possible, and using the cash flow to buy more properties. Leverage to the max.

The leverage concept may work during an inflationary period when prices are rising, but when the music stops and the cycle heads the other direction, watch out. Downturns in the real estate cycle have bankrupted many overleveraged real estate investors. Leverage is an integral part of real estate investing, but we must be very prudent in its use. We will cover leverage in more detail later in the book.

We have just been through one of the worst down cycles I have seen in my real estate career and many overleveraged real estate investors have suffered as a result. So a balanced approach to the use of leverage is important. And, as we will discuss, paying off real estate debt as fast as you can, will lead to a high margin of safety in your real estate investing.

With this new and exciting concept of paying off real

estate debt quickly fresh in my mind, I immediately began to refocus my real estate investing goals. Taking this approach has allowed me to weather the ups and downs of the real estate market cycles and to enjoy some of the fruits of real estate investing success.

Real estate cannot be lost or stolen,
nor can it be carried away.
Purchased with common sense, paid for in full,
and managed with reasonable care,
it is about the safest investment in the world.
Franklin D. Roosevelt

~ 3 ~
A Mentor Should be
Your First Acquisition

Let me share with you how I met my first mentor Frank Takes who I talked about in the Dedications and Acknowledgments section at the beginning of this book.

A simple good deed made my path to real estate investing much smoother than it would have been otherwise.

As I mentioned in Chapter 1, after dropping out of college I was working as a church janitor in Cedar Rapids, Iowa. Across the street from the church was one of the main offices of John Zachar Realtors. Frequently, I'd see a pristine white Cadillac pull up in front of the real estate office and I'd think to myself, *Someday, I'm going to have a car like that.*

One day while I was mowing the lawn at the church, I watched as the man who owned the white Cadillac came out to his car, put his briefcase on the car's roof, got into his car and prepared to drive away. I stopped what I was doing and ran to retrieve his briefcase for him before he drove off. We started to talk, and it wasn't too long before the company Frank worked for, John Zachar Realtors, encouraged me to trade in my mop and bucket for a career in residential real estate sales.

I've known Frank now for over 35 years and he is an enthusiastic, caring man who loves to see others succeed. Frank helped me set goals for my real estate sales career and challenged me to begin investing in real estate.

In one of the first meetings I had with Frank after joining John Zachar Realtors, he gave me a copy of the book *Think and Grow Rich* by Napoleon Hill. He then instructed me to go across the street from our office to Pinckney's Drug Store and purchase a 19- cent spiral note book to begin writing down my goals. The counsel and direction I received from Frank regarding goal setting and real estate investing at twenty years old pointed my life in a new and exciting direction. As I look back now at where my life has gone, I must say that this was a transforming moment. The influence of good mentors is invaluable. It can and will change your life. Good mentors can expose you to ideas you may have never considered. Mentors also provide encouragement that will give you confidence in your ability to achieve your goals. I must side track here with a short, related story.

Pinckney's Drug Store, where I purchased my spiral note book, was located on First Avenue in Cedar Rapids, Iowa in the Town and Country Shopping Center. The Town and Country Shopping Center was the first shopping center developed by the Bucksbaum brothers whose company, General Growth Properties, grew into one of the largest shopping center development companies in the United States. Later in this book we will talk about finding one property type to specialize in to enhance your investing success. The Bucksbaum brothers' specialization in shopping center development brought them great success over the years.

Because of Frank's encouragement, I read many books about real estate investing which, in effect, were also like mentors to me. By them, I learned how and was inspired to set goals for my life. Let me encourage you to do the same! For your enrichment, I have provided a list of the books I've read, from those with the classic, tried and true principles to the newer editions that bring a fresh perspective. You'll find the list in the back of the book in Appendix A. Read as much as you can and glean from the experts. Learn from their mistakes and successes. Let them be part of your mentoring team!

Not only have my mentors been kind enough to share with me how they achieved success in life and real estate investing, they have also shared with me the life lessons they learned when things did not work out as planned. Through these relationships, I was able to observe firsthand the transactions my mentors entered into and how they negotiated and structured their real estate purchases. Some even opened up their financial records so I could get a feel for how their real estate portfolios had grown through the years. Over time, I developed some great friendships with these folks and have entered into partnerships with a number of them on real estate investments.

Most of my mentors had compiled real estate investment portfolios worth between $1 million and $10 million by the time I met them. As the years passed, I have watched as the value of their real estate holdings have grown. A number of them likely have real estate holdings now in excess of $20 million. It's amazing what happens when you combine real estate with time!

While I met Frank through a good deed, you don't need a chance encounter to find a mentor. I have found that most people, when approached properly, are happy to share their path to success with others. It all boils down to being respectful—both in your approach and in the amount of their time you take up—and appreciative of the advice you receive.

Find a number of real estate investors in your community that you can get to know and learn from; soak up the information they share with you like a sponge. Having good mentors is one of the real secrets to success in real estate investing.

If you want to be rich, only listen to the people who have started with nothing and amassed a fortune. Only someone who's done it can show you how to do it.
                                        Terence Storm

~ 4 ~
# What Is Your Emotional Trigger?

To achieve my goals in life, I learned early on that I needed to identify what I call my emotional triggers. What deep issues energize me to get up in the morning and work hard to achieve my goals? What are my real underlying motivations to succeed? Each of us needs to ask ourselves these questions. We need to find out what drives us. So ask yourself: What are the deep, emotional triggers in my life that will keep me focused on reaching my goals no matter how great the obstacles I encounter?

It's been said that money can't buy happiness. That is definitely true, and I know this for certain: money can't buy motivation. I have seen many people try real estate investing in their desire to get rich. Each time, they encounter a few challenges, and their real estate investing career comes to an end. The desire just to own a lot of real estate and to be wealthy simply isn't enough. There needs to be a more powerful, more compelling reason to keep each of us on track to achieve our goals.

I have talked with many successful real estate investors through the years and have sought to discover their emotional triggers. Most of them are extremely private people who look like ordinary folks on the outside. Inside each of them, though, there is a finely tuned emotional engine that is driven to succeed.

What are some emotional triggers? None of them are

direct reasons to invest in real estate, but they are factors that can really spark the inner fire in people. Here are a few examples:

- You were a nerd in high school and want to prove to your classmates and the world that you are somebody.
- Your family moved from rental home to rental home while you were growing up, and you have a deep desire to have the stability that comes with owning real property.
- Your mother and father never thought you would amount to anything, and you are going to prove to them that you have succeeded in life.
- You never went to college, and you desperately want your children to have the benefits of a college education.
- You will do whatever it takes to retire at a young age.
- You struggled academically in high school or flunked out of your freshman year of college, but told yourself you would succeed at something.
- One of your long time friends has become a successful real estate investor and you believe that if he can do it, then so can you.
- You grew up poor and have a deep desire for some of the material comforts in life.
- You admire a financially successful person and want to be like them.

These are just a few of an unlimited number of

emotional triggers. Some of these types of desires are in each of us. The key is to think about the experiences in our lives that have impacted us and identify what really motivates us.

Not too long ago, I went to the grand opening of a new bank branch. Many of the bank's customers in attendance were high net-worth individuals, including some successful real estate investors. I approached one of the investors whom I had known for some time and asked him what inner desires had motivated him to achieve his real estate investing success.

He shared with me that he had worked for a large insurance company before becoming a real estate investor. Over the years as he worked at the company he said that he looked around the office at his co-workers and thought about where they would each end up financially when they retired. Most of them, he realized, would end up with a small pension and a gold watch. He said, "I am a competitive guy, and I decided that I wanted more than that."

This is a common theme I have found among successful real estate investors. Most of them have a strong competitive spirit. They want to accomplish something with their talents and skills. Oftentimes, they are competing not against others, but rather to achieve their own lofty goals. They want to make their mark on the world and real estate investing is one way to accomplish that.

Another investor I know comes from a family who owns and operates a very successful multimillion-dollar regional business. This investor told me he wanted to prove that he had obtained his success on his own, not as a result of the wealth that had been passed on to him by his family.

One of my best customers through the years told me he was driven by the fear of being poor. He had grown up in a very poor family and didn't want to end up living like his parents had. I can relate somewhat to that emotional trigger. As I mentioned earlier, I grew up in a small Iowa farm town, and my parents were both teachers. Both of them enjoyed their work and put in long hours to support my two sisters and me. We were not poor and our needs were met. My wife, Kae, came from a similar family; her father was a Lutheran pastor, and her mother stayed at home with the children. We were both fortunate to come from loving, supportive families of modest means. However, with so modest an upbringing, I eventually developed a desire to achieve a greater level of financial security than I had known.

While launching my career in real estate sales, I began learning from my mentor Frank about real estate investing and wealth accumulation. This was the first time I had been exposed to many of these concepts. I soon realized that both my parents and my in-laws had focused most of their lives on their work and family, with little attention given to their retirement and financial future. Perhaps they did, but I don't recall it being a topic of conversation at the dinner table.

With what I was learning from Frank, it was clear to me that if I wanted to end up with a substantial net worth at retirement, it was something to which I would need to devote some time and energy. It was not just going to happen. Kae remembers me coming home one night early in my career and saying, "I am not going to end up at retirement like our parents. I want something more to show for my life than a house and a pension."

Now, let's keep this in perspective. Building wealth and possessing a large estate doesn't in itself bring contentment and happiness. While I had a desire to accomplish more financially than my parents and in-laws, both of those couples have lived enjoyable, fulfilling lives. I'm a little biased on this next point, but I think they did a darn good job raising their kids as well, and I learned plenty about life from them that has made me a better husband, father and person. Keep in mind that financial resources are just one measure of accomplishment. It is the accomplishments themselves that bring the truest satisfaction, not necessarily the financial resources that may come as a result.

Finding and understanding the deep emotional triggers in my own life has helped me set and achieve many financial goals. I encourage you to search your inner self and try to identify honestly what drives you. What are the deep emotional desires that can power you forward to achieve your goals? What will move you closer to becoming a successful real estate investor? The answer to that question could be the key to your success. At a minimum, it will keep you going when things get tough.

*Singleness of purpose is one of the chief essentials
for success in life, no matter what may be one's aim.*
John D. Rockefeller

*If you want to be successful, it's just this simple.
Know what you are doing.
Love what you are doing.
And believe in what you are doing.*
Will Rogers

~ 5 ~
Where Do I Get the Cash
to Get Started?

It is never too late to start investing in real estate, regardless of where you are in life. It's just like a lot of things; where there's a will, there's a way!

When I first started investing in real estate, I borrowed some of the cash required on private notes to get the down payment I needed. Then I worked to pay off those notes from property cash flow or any other means. Couple that with a seller-provided note and deed of trust for 90% of the purchase price, and I was on my way. Since then, I have raised capital by any legal means necessary. I sold my personal cars and one time I sold our family boat to generate the cash needed for my real estate investments. I also refinanced my home a number of times over the years to get investment capital. I've done what I've needed to do in order to make a real estate investment.

If you are young and just starting out, it *might* make sense to borrow money from friends or against your house in order to pay for a real estate investment. However, in today's economic climate, I would be more inclined to find partners to put up a prudent amount of equity so that together we can pursue investments with lower debt and less stress.

Probably the most stress-free option is to find a

partner who will put up all of the cash if you do the work. I have done this successfully many times. Your partner gets a good return on his initial investment, and once he makes his money back, the two of you can split the profits. Of course, it's incumbent upon you to make sure the investment is solid, and to manage the property so the investor gets a solid return. If you do your job, the relationship will be mutually beneficial.

Here's an example of how such an arrangement might be structured. The investor puts up the down payment and gets an 8% preferred annual return that will be paid from cash flow and the eventual sale of the property. After the investor has received his initial investment back plus an 8% annual return, the remaining profits are split between the two of you.

The split will depend on a number of variables: the type of property, the level of risk, how much work you do as manager, and how motivated you are to find an investment partner. The split can range from 50-50 to 80-20. The more experience and the more success you have, the better you'll be able to define the relationship.

There is an old real estate maxim that says *if you find a great deal, you will have no problem coming up with the money.* I have found that to be true. There are always people with money looking for the proverbial good deal, and you can be rewarded for being a deal finder. It's tougher when you are getting started and have no track record, but the more successful investments you make, the easier it will be to find the partners you need.

While this chapter addresses the question, "Where do I get the cash to get started?" I would be remiss if I didn't mention one other key factor, which I will discuss further in the next chapter. I have observed many successful investors through the years, and many of them have one trait in common: they live very frugal lives. By living below their means, they are able to save up the cash to invest. Examine your lifestyle and look for places to adjust your priorities and make it a priority to save some cash to invest. You must continue this practice as you begin to experience some investment success. Keep on living frugally and you will be able to move on to bigger and more substantial investments. Are you willing to make some changes in order to reach your goals?

In the early days of my investing career, I didn't have a lot of cash, and it was tough to stick to this program. As I got started, sometimes I had to sell a smaller property at a profit to generate money to purchase a larger property. When I did sell something, however, I was careful not to spend my working capital or profits.

There's a somewhat barbaric saying that some real estate investors use that says, "*Don't eat your children if you want them to grow up.*" In other words, don't spend your investment capital if you want it to keep growing. This is where discipline comes in. Many people sell a property, get that big check and buy a car or something along those lines. You must use your investment capital wisely to make additional investments, not just spend it.

It isn't easy. I struggle now and again with the temptation to give myself a little reward from my investment profits. I'm human, and I've succumbed to that temptation before. About 15 years ago, Kae and I sold an office building that we had owned for some time and received a rather large check at closing. We desperately needed to replace one of our cars and after some consideration we decided to pay cash for a new car with a portion of the proceeds. It still bothers me a bit when I think about putting all that cash into a vehicle; I don't like sinking money into depreciating assets!

It might have been a better long term decision to take the cash and invest it in a property that would produce steady cash flow, then finance the car and use the cash flow from the property to cover all or most of the car payment. However, at that point in life I had decided to never finance the purchase of a car again, so paying cash for the car worked best.

To sum up, review the resources that you have available to help you get started investing. If you don't have resources that you can convert to cash, you will need to be creative and look for properties that you can get into with little or no cash. High leverage can equate to high risk. If you are averse to some risk in getting started, search out a partner who can put up the cash. Be persistent and you will find a way to get started!

I believe that thrift is essential to well-ordered living.
                                        John D. Rockefeller

~ 6 ~
Lifestyle Changes

Most of us work hard to settle into a lifestyle much like that of our parents—what we envision as the norm. We start with that lifestyle, then change with the times and do the things our peers do. This lifestyle might include a trip to Starbucks or our favorite coffee shop once or even twice a day, which is far from unusual in this day and age. To achieve our financial goals, however, we need to be different from the status quo. We may need to adjust our priorities and make some lifestyle changes to achieve our goals.

A few stories come to mind when thinking about people who have altered their lifestyles to reach their goals in real estate.

One starts with The Hutton Settlement, an orphanage in the Spokane area that started in the 1900s and has always generated the income for its operations through real estate investments. A no-nonsense man named Bob Revel managed the Hutton Settlement for 40-some years. Several years ago he relayed a story to me.

At one time, the Hutton Settlement owned an office building that was leased to IBM. The building was constructed on a hillside and includes a parking area under the building that ends where the structure and the hillside meet. A number of years ago, some of the IBM employees told Bob that someone was actually living under the building in that space. Bob investigated, and sure enough, just out of sight under the building were a couple of wood pallets with a sleeping bag and a few personal belongings on them.

Later that night he waited for the trespasser to return. After a couple of hours, a man appeared and entered his makeshift home under the building. Bob approached and asked the man why he was living there, adding that the tenants had complained and that he couldn't live there anymore. The man said he understood, but told Bob he had a nursing degree and had taken a job a few blocks away at Deaconess Medical Center. He said he was living under the building so that he could save money for the down payment on a home. Apparently, the man showered at the hospital each day and ate most meals in the hospital cafeteria. Bob let him stay a few more days but requested that he find a new place to live.

Am I suggesting we all sleep outside so we can save money to buy real estate? Of course not, but I do want you to think outside the box. Here's a young man who made a huge adjustment—indeed, a huge sacrifice—to eventually achieve his dream of owning a home. My point is that all of us need to review our lifestyle choices from time to time and see if they are supporting the goals we want to achieve. Many times, by adjusting our lifestyle, we can reach the financial goals that will propel us forward and provide the peace of mind we desire.

A few years ago, we had a temporary employee working in my office. She was in her mid-20s and told me how she and her husband wanted to own a home in the country. However, they couldn't afford any homes they found near Spokane. Instead of giving up, they bought 20 acres of timbered land about 45 miles north of Spokane and built a modest log cabin there. In the beginning, they didn't have electricity or running water, but they did have a large garden that provided much of the food they ate. They were thrilled to own their own place in the country and had adjusted their lifestyle to meet their goals.

One more example of radical lifestyle adjustment is a Korean immigrant who moved to Spokane many years ago and got a job as a cook at a Chinese restaurant. He ate all his meals there and, rather than rent an apartment, he slept on bags of rice in the basement of the restaurant. This allowed him to save all his money and ultimately purchase a convenience store.

These examples are extreme, but I share them so that you can open your mind to the possibilities of change and adjustment in your own life. I know many successful real estate investors who lived very modest and frugal lives so that they could accumulate cash for real estate investing.

Here's a more tangible example from my own experience: My kids spend what appears to me to be a substantial portion of their income on fast food and expensive coffee drinks. For their generation, their behavior is the norm. When I go out to eat, however, I drink water. My folks didn't buy soft drinks when I was growing up, so I have never been a big soda drinker. I never acquired the taste for coffee either. If you want to melt Haagen Dazs coffee-flavored ice cream, I'll gladly drink that, but otherwise, coffee isn't for me! Believe it or not, by **not** drinking soda and coffee, I have likely saved enough money for a number of the investments I have made through the years!

Maybe you're one of those daily Starbucks visitors. A

typical latte costs between \$3 and \$4. For the sake of this example, let's say you spend \$3 every day at Starbucks. That adds up to over \$1,000 a year! I have nothing against Starbucks; they are a great company. I am also not saying everyone should give up drinking coffee. What I am trying to do is get you to recognize opportunities to adjust your lifestyle. All of us can make a few adjustments and end up with a nice investment nest egg in no time.

If you want to reach your real estate investing goals, examine ways you can adjust your lifestyle to free up some cash for investing. Most people are able to do this if they put their minds to it. Ask yourself these questions: Where are the savings opportunities in my budget? What do I need to change about my lifestyle?

It's really all about establishing your priorities. What is most important? If getting started in real estate investing is really a priority for you, then make the needed adjustments to your life and get started! You'll be well on your way to meeting your financial goals and enjoying the fruits of your labors before you know it!

The time to save is now. When a dog gets a bone,
he doesn't go out and make a down payment
on a bigger bone. He buries the one he's got.
                    Will Rogers

~ 7 ~
Financial Capacity and Reserves

When I talk to people about real estate investing, one concept they often don't understand is **financial capacity**. Actually, it's a simple concept to comprehend, and it's crucial to successful investing, even more so today than it ever has been in the past.

My definition of financial capacity is *"having the ability to make mortgage payments and cover other costs associated with owning real estate from personal cash flow and savings when the income from the property is insufficient to do so."* You must have the financial capacity to make it through unforeseeable events, such as a tenant who unexpectedly goes out of business and leaves you with a mortgage payment to make each month, or members of a partnership who can no longer make their payments.

Whether you have partners or you are the sole investor, the question is, do you have the financial capacity to make the required payments? If that question goes unasked or the answer is no, trouble might follow.

When I think of financial capacity troubles, three examples come immediately to mind. In each case, a retired couple purchased a single- or two-tenant building to provide a portion of their retirement income. Each of these couples had accumulated wealth through the years, but none of them had gained much experience in real estate investing. Each couple purchased a sizable investment property to provide income for their retirement. Thinking that they were taking a conservative approach to investing they all made a substantial down payment on the properties they bought. Even with a large amount of equity in the property, they still relied on their tenants to pay rent and provide the income needed to cover their monthly mortgage payments and have funds left over to provide for their retirement living expenses.

The first couple bought a 20,000 square foot office building on a main arterial in an industrial area. It was well built with plenty of parking, and had two creditworthy tenants that filled it. They paid $1.75 million for the property and made a down payment of $900,000. They borrowed $850,000 and had monthly payments of $6,590 a month. After the rent was collected and all building operating expenses were paid, the monthly net operating income was about $12,500. This was more than enough to cover the mortgage payment of $6,590. As a result, the couple had cash flow from the investment of $5,910 per month, or $70,920 per year. This income provided a significant part of what they counted on each month to live on:

Monthly Net Operating Income	$12,500
Monthly Mortgage Payment	$ 6,590
Monthly Cash Flow	$ 5,910

That was all well and good, until one of the leases expired, and the tenant with the expired lease moved out of the building. Stung by the loss of income from the tenant who moved out and feeling somewhat desperate, the couple became inflexible and difficult to deal with when the second tenant's lease came up for renewal. They couldn't come to terms on a lease renewal, and the second tenant moved out as well. Now, rather than earning $5,910 a month, they needed to come up with $6,590 a month to cover their mortgage payment. In addition to the mortgage payment, they also needed to begin paying all the expenses required to keep the property operating.

This couple was relying on their investment to provide income and support their lifestyle in retirement. At this stage of life, they didn't have the financial capacity to shell out $6,590 a month plus operating expenses. They also faced the costs associated with filling the building with new tenants. Those costs include leasing commissions to a real estate broker to find new tenants, and improvements to the building to make it attractive to prospective tenants. These are normal expenses a real estate investor will incur over the life of an investment, but some investors don't adequately factor them in when they purchase a property. The couple was not prepared for this financial setback.

After spending a lot of time and effort trying unsuccessfully to find new tenants, the couple had to consider selling the property in order to rid themselves of the negative cash flow problem. Eventually, they sold the building for $1.25 million, losing $500,000 of their retirement savings.

I had mentioned three instances where couples had invested money in real estate in retirement. In the other two examples, the couples suffered similar fates as the first. Through inexperience and poor counsel from real estate brokers, all three couples put themselves in positions that were beyond their financial capacities and severely strained their personal finances.

What should they have done differently? First, since they didn't have the financial capacity to cover the payments on a totally vacant building, they should have purchased less expensive properties so they didn't have to carry any debt. If they were comfortable with some debt, they should have bought multi-tenant buildings where the risk of losing all of the tenants at once was greatly reduced. With a five or six-tenant building, for example, they might have to spend more time or money on management, but they would have less overall vacancy risk.

Another thing that would have been helpful is to have established a **reserve fund** for the unexpected. This is not just prudent, but crucial, to successful investing. Tenants move out, roofs need repair, real estate taxes increase, heating and air conditioning units need to be replaced, buildings need to be painted, and so on. In real estate, you must always expect the unexpected. Having a reserve account for such unanticipated expenses is a wise approach to ensuring you have the financial capacity to invest in a property.

How much should you have in reserves? I recommend a minimum of one month's operating expenses. Then, if for some reason your tenant or tenants pay their rent late, you can still cover your mortgage payment and other expenses. It would be even better to have funds to cover six months' worth of expenses in a reserve account. With time and experience, you will get a feel for what each property requires, as well as your tenants' rent payment patterns.

The longer you own a piece of property, the more you also become aware of the capital improvements needed to maintain the property in top condition. I am extremely conscientious about keeping my properties well-maintained. Tenants stay longer and such high quality properties command top dollar when they are sold. If they are not maintained properly, then more expensive repairs may eventually be required.

Take asphalt parking lots for example. If they are seal coated regularly every three to five years they will usually have a long life. If they are not properly cared for the asphalt begins to crack and break up over time. The resulting cost of repaving can be very expensive."

One way to expand financial capacity for investments is to form partnerships with likeminded investors. When I started putting together real estate investment partnerships, there was one key point I figured out early on: in the case of buying land make sure your partners can make their payments. After hearing a few war stories from one of my mentors about partners who couldn't pay, I knew I didn't want partners calling me after a deal was done and telling me they couldn't hold up their end of the agreement. I was very careful to choose partners who could easily make the monthly payments or had the financial capacity to participate in the partnership.

I would try to bring them into the partnership with a monthly payment that was half what they could afford each month. This gave me the peace of mind that they could make good on their commitments, but it also helped account for the financial ups and downs we would possibly encounter, and ensure we had the financial capacity to invest together.

I will talk more about partnerships in Chapter 21, but for now, remember this: Whether you invest with partners or independently, you must first give serious consideration to your financial capacity before investing. Determine realistically what your financial capacity is and plan for the unplanned expenses by establishing a reserve account. Believe me, this will make your investing career much less stressful and much more enjoyable.

You only have to do a few things right in your life
so long as you don't do too many things wrong.
                                   Warren Buffett

~ 8 ~
What If I Live in L.A.?

Many of us are fortunate to live in communities where real estate investments, residential and commercial, are affordable. In Spokane, Washington, you can shop for a commercial building in the $250,000 to $500,000 range and have plenty of options to choose from. It used to be common to find a building for $100,000 to $250,000 in our market. It's still possible to find lower priced properties like that, but it takes some hunting. Competition from small business owners who want to own and occupy their own building tends to drive prices up on many lower priced properties.

But what if you live in Los Angeles or New York City? Or anyplace else where real estate investments of less than $500,000 are nearly impossible to find? Consider looking in less expensive markets outside your community that are stable and growing.

There is an economic principle that talks about capital flowing to where it is most productive. We have seen that in play in the Spokane market, where a couple in California discovers they can sell their home for $800,000 and buy a larger home in Spokane for $250,000. They then have $550,000 in cash to fund their retirement or start a small business.

The principle of capital flowing to where it is most productive will eventually happen in cities like Detroit, where real estate prices have hit rock bottom and have nowhere to go but up. In the late 2000s, I received an advertisement for an auction that offered a block of 175 single-family homes in the Detroit area at an average price of $3,500 per home. They might have set the starting bid low in an effort to attract more bidders, but it still serves as a sign of just how depressed prices are in that market.

Remember, when looking for less-expensive markets, the key is to look at communities that are stable and growing. You can always find cheap real estate to invest in, but you want to do so in a market that has potential for growth. Recently, I was visiting my family in Iowa and ran across an advertisement for a three-bedroom home in a small town near the Iowa-Minnesota border. The home was priced at $15,000! I took the ad back to Spokane with me and circulated it around my office. One employee was so amazed at this apparent great value that she actually gave some thought to moving to Iowa. It was a great value, but it was not in a community with any prospects for future growth. Many Midwest towns are shrinking in size, and young people in that particular part of the country are moving to Des Moines or Minneapolis to find jobs. The house would be cheap, but as an investment, it likely would be difficult to rent out and probably would not appreciate much over time.

If you need to go outside of your market to invest, do your homework carefully. Study demographic information to find cities with steady growth. Each year, Forbes Magazine publishes a list of the best places to live, and the list is usually filled with small to mid-sized growing communities. You'll want to dig deeper than that, however, and look for markets where there is potential for job and population growth.

There are real estate investment promoters who focus on growth statistics and other demographic information to guide real estate investors. For a fee, they agree to provide prospective buyers with this information, and they also arrange buying trips, mostly focused on single-family home investments. On these trips, the promoters fly potential investors in and put them on chartered buses, giving them tours of cities with depressed real estate prices. I have a couple of friends who have joined these groups and have gone on these trips. It is one thing to buy a commercial building or a multi-unit apartment building and hire a property manager in a city far away. It is quite another thing to buy one single-family rental house far from your home. Yes, you can find good property managers in another city to manage a rental house, but it's difficult to justify that expense with one small investment. To own a far-from-home investment property for which you don't have a manager is risky and can be expensive.

I know a number of real estate investors who own properties outside of our market area. Most of them are not willing to travel more than half of a day to get to their investments. Their time is valuable and they work to keep their investments within a manageable distance.

One word of caution: A story is told about a farmer who sold his farm to travel the world in search of riches. He came home broke and weary, only to find out that diamonds had been discovered on his former farm.

While looking outside your own market might bring the investments you seek, remember that you're doing so because the price of entry in your market is high, not because the opportunity is better elsewhere. There are great deals to be had in any market. If you look long enough at enough properties, you can always find a great deal.

So, check out the real estate investment options that are close to home. If the barriers to entry are too high, begin looking for growing communities with investment real estate prices that you can afford. You never know: Spokane, Washington might even be on your list!

Every person who invests in well-selected real estate
in a growing section of a prosperous community adopts
the surest and safest method of becoming independent,
for real estate is the basis of wealth.
Theodore Roosevelt

~ 9 ~
Picking a Good Broker

Even if you have developed your skills as a real estate investor, you will benefit from the assistance of a knowledgeable commercial real estate broker. Picking a good broker with the right skill set is a key component of successful investing. Just like selecting an attorney, an accountant, or any other professional service provider, you need to do your homework and carefully select a broker who is best suited to assist you with your investment objectives.

Quality real estate brokers typically specialize in one type of property. They usually work in retail, industrial, office or apartments. Brokers might have a major and a minor, so to speak, but the top brokers are usually market experts in their specialty. They develop a vast amount of knowledge about the property type they specialize in. It is difficult to be a generalist in real estate investing because there's just too much important information to master for each property type. An investment broker can use his skills to analyze any type of investment property, but each property type has its own nuances and unique features. It takes years of experience to build up the specialized knowledge that's needed to successfully invest in specific types of commercial real estate.

So, to find the best commercial real estate brokers,

talk with other real estate investors, bankers, CPAs, and commercial real estate appraisers. You want to find a broker who has a track record in the property type in which you want to invest. It helps if there is a personality fit as well, but that's not the most important ingredient. It's most important to find a broker who has a reputation for having integrity, being fair, working hard, and ultimately, finding good properties.

The top investment brokers are always talking to property owners and are able to find properties for their customers that aren't actively listed for sale on the market. A study was done by CBRE (Coldwell Banker Richard Ellis) that determined that 6–7% of the investment real estate in the U.S. is for sale at any given time. The average broker will focus his or her energy on this much-picked-over inventory. The top brokers will focus on all the properties in the market, both the properties that are for sale and those that aren't for sale.

About six years ago, an investor client of mine called and told me his family had just sold a piece of property and would be receiving about $1.7 million in proceeds from the sale. They wanted to complete a Section 1031 tax-deferred exchange and wanted to find a replacement investment property in the $2.5 million to $4 million price range. An IRS Section 1031 exchange would allow them to transfer their equity from the property they had sold into a new property and defer paying capital gains taxes.

Initially, I put together a package of properties which were currently listed for sale that fit their criteria. Then I started to think about other buildings not on the market that might be available. I remembered one building that had been for sale a few years earlier, but it had been pulled off the market. This building had high vacancies, and the owner wanted to lease it up to increase the property's income—and thereby, its value—before he sold it. I called the broker who had formerly had that property for sale and asked if the owners might possibly be ready to sell. He said that he and the owners were working with a tenant who was going to lease the majority of the vacant space in the building. Once that tenant signed a lease, the owner planned to put the building back on the market.

I quickly called my client and arranged a tour of the property. After touring the building my client made an offer to purchase the property contingent on the pending lease being signed. He then did his due diligence on the property, and everything checked out to his satisfaction. Shortly thereafter, the prospective tenant signed the lease, and the $3.55 million sale was finalized. We were fortunate to get a foot in the door before the property was put on the market. So finding a broker who will search out deals for you that no one else knows about is a key to enhancing your investing opportunities and success.

When you hire a broker to work for you, make sure you clearly define your working relationship. The real estate licensing laws in most states require that brokers explain agency relationships to all potential clients before they begin working together. In other words, the broker must explain who he is going to represent. If you are actively looking for investment real estate, you want a knowledgeable broker who will represent your interests. The broker who has the property listed represents the seller. In some states, a broker can act as a dual agent and "facilitate" a transaction for a buyer and a seller, but the best situation is to have a broker looking out for your interests exclusively as the buyer.

Clearly define your expectations of the working relationship. The best brokers will be pro-active in defining the relationship. If the broker doesn't bring this up or doesn't want to talk about it, ask hard questions to clarify and establish the relationship you will have with the broker.

Make sure you understand how a broker or salesperson will be compensated before you get started. Brokers work exclusively on a commission basis. The amount of a commission varies from market to market and also by the size of the deal. Brokers representing buyers only get paid if they are party to a transaction and get a deal closed. Commissions are most commonly paid by the sellers of a property, but can be paid by the buyer if that is your agreement with the broker. Commissions are usually shared between the listing broker and the selling broker but that is not always the case. So again, determine your working relationship with your broker up front so that you are both clear about what is expected from each of you.

Many brokers will ask that you work with them on an exclusive basis. They request this to make sure they will be compensated if you buy a property after they spend months showing you properties and educating you on investment real estate. It only makes sense.

That said, some sophisticated investors prefer to work with brokers on a non-exclusive basis. They want to leave themselves open to working with a number of quality investment brokers. When doing so, these investors make sure a broker gets paid if they buy a property that has been submitted to them by that broker.

Whatever you do, make sure you do your best to ensure that the broker who assists you gets compensated for his or her efforts. If you are fair with a broker, that broker will bring you the good deals he's bound to come across. If you don't back him up to get paid he will take his good deals to the clients who will make sure he does get paid. A good investment broker can help you build a very profitable investment portfolio.

Risk comes from not knowing what you are doing.
Warren Buffett

~ Notes ~

~ 10 ~
A Prudent Process

The Webster's Dictionary definition of **prudent** is *"wise and judicious in practical affairs."* It defines **process** as *"a systematic series of actions directed at some end."*

Making solid real estate investments involves going through what I refer to as a **prudent process**. A prudent process involves wisely walking through a series of action steps to come to a carefully evaluated conclusion—either *"Yes, this property is a wise investment,"* or *"No, this isn't a smart buy."* Big decisions like investing in real estate should never be done in haste. An appropriate amount of time should be taken to review and process all the information related to a property before you make the decision to buy.

For a number of years I worked on marketing and selling some excess land parcels for one of the largest privately owned companies in Washington State. This was a family owned business and the real estate decisions at the company were made by two brothers. It did not take too long to figure out that the brothers exercised a prudent process for making their real estate decisions.

Whenever we needed to meet on a major issue, one of the brothers would set a meeting with me that was usually scheduled in the afternoon. We would review the information that needed to be acted on and then he would say, "Let me talk to my brother and I will call you tomorrow." This was the brothers' prudent process for decision making. They never made a big decision without conferring between themselves and thinking about their course of action over night.

Many years ago, I received a call from a client named Fred. I had helped Fred acquire an office building for his business a few years earlier. Fred told me that he and his sister had inherited some property in California. They were in the process of selling that property and wanted to do a **tax-deferred exchange**, taking the money from the California sale and putting it into an income property in the Spokane area where they lived. We will talk about tax-deferred exchanges in more depth later in the book, but in the simplest terms, an exchange allows a property owner to defer all or part of the capital-gains from the sale of a property. To do so, the proceeds from the sale must be used to acquire another in-kind investment property within a prescribed time frame.

Fred and his sister were due to receive $450,000 cash from the property sale in California. Their goal was to invest this money in commercial real estate that would provide a steady, dependable income stream. We determined a multi-tenant office or retail building would be their best option. They didn't want to borrow any more than 50% of the purchase price of the property, so their goal was to find one or more properties with values totaling up to about $900,000.

I then shared with Fred how we would go through a prudent process to find the best possible property or properties to meet his and his sister's investment objectives. I told them this would likely take six to nine months. This time frame will vary widely depending upon the city and marketplace you are in and the number of properties that you consider.

At the beginning of this process, I gathered information on nearly 50 properties actively listed for sale by brokers and by property owners.

I told Fred that together we would review the packages and information on these properties and sort out 20 to 25 properties to physically inspect. From there, we would choose a number of properties on which to begin making offers. At any time during the process, we would continue to consider other properties that became available.

We visited 27 properties and wrote offers on five of them. We let the sellers know we had limited funds and that we had made multiple offers. By making multiple offers, we hoped to create competition between the sellers and gauge better which properties would be the best values. Also, it gave Fred and his sister back-up options. If one property didn't work out or if someone came in with a better offer, we wouldn't be starting back at square one. This isn't a luxury we would be afforded in a white-hot market, but it worked for us in Spokane at that time.

Fred and his sister had two directions they could go as a result of the multiple offers: one property that could be purchased for about $800,000 or two others that totaled about $725,000.

After a few rounds of negotiation and a review of the benefits and disadvantages of each option, they elected to tie up the $800,000 property. This is when the real work begins: check out all aspects of the property during a **contingency period** to determine if you want to pass or play. A contingency period is a specified period of time that a seller provides to a buyer, usually at no cost, to check out the property and determine if the buyer is ready to go forward with the purchase. In most cases a buyer will ask for a 30- to 60-day contingency period to study a property. In most markets, sellers will allow a buyer to tie up a piece of property for a contingency period with earnest money that is refundable if the buyer does not remove any contingencies. If it is a seller's market, the buyer may have to pay some nonrefundable money to hold a property off the market.

During the contingency period the study of the property is called **due diligence**. Due diligence is the final part of the prudent process. We will cover due diligence in detail in the next chapter, but suffice it to say, due diligence has one of two outcomes. Any problems that are discovered are easily resolved, and the property moves into closing. Or, problems can't be resolved, and the buyer passes and begins to look for another property.

Fred and his sister finalized their prudent process by completing the due diligence on the property under contract. Everything checked out to their satisfaction and they closed on the purchase of the property.

Contrast that example to a phone call I received from a lady a couple of years ago who lived in a farm town about 100 miles from Spokane. She called me on a Thursday and asked if I could assist her in purchasing an investment property that weekend. She said that her parents' estate had just been settled, and she would be receiving a check for $200,000 the following week. She had decided she wanted to invest the money in commercial real estate. She said she wanted to get a property bought that weekend so she could quickly start receiving income on her investment. I asked her if she had previously purchased any commercial real estate. She said no. As tactfully as possible, I suggested that she consider going through a prudent process to invest her money properly.

After further discussion it was obvious that she was not interested in my counsel. I could tell that this was a train wreck ready to happen and tried to bow out gracefully. As the conversation came to an end, she told me she would need to find a real professional who knew the market well enough to find her something to buy that weekend. I wished her well and said goodbye. You know the old saying, "Haste makes waste."

If the prudent process sounds like it takes a lot of time, it is because it does. But when you're looking to invest your hard earned money to buy commercial real estate, you want to make sure you are carefully covering all the bases and making a well thought out decision.

The more properties you consider and analyze during a prudent process, the better decision you will be able to make. Take your time and carefully examine all aspects of each property to make sure that the property meets or exceeds your investment goals.

Going through this process on many properties will give you a great deal of valuable market knowledge and will sharpen your decision making skills. The more times you go through the prudent process, the more comfortable you will be each time you do it—and the more successful you will be in choosing high performing real estate investments.

In good deals the numbers work.
In bad deals they don't.
                              Ken McElroy

~ 11 ~
Do Your Homework:
The Wisdom of Due Diligence

You've gone through the prudent process to select a good investment property. You've made an offer on the property and received an acceptance from the seller. Now, the real work begins. It's time to do your homework, or **due diligence,** which I briefly introduced in the previous chapter.

Due diligence is the in-depth research you will do on the property you've contracted to buy. There are two main goals in due diligence. The first is to verify the information you have received on the property from the seller and the seller's real estate agent to determine if the information is accurate and reliable. Your second goal is to gather additional information about the property that will help you determine if the property is one you want to purchase. You want to gather all the information on the property you can so that you clearly understand everything there is to know about it.

The tasks involved in due diligence fall into four basic categories: financial, physical, technical and practical. I'll go into more detail on these categories and provide a checklist at the end of this chapter. Having a good checklist helps you remember to cover all your bases.

How in depth do you need to go? Try and find out more about the property than the seller himself knows. Property owners tend to get complacent as the years pass and can lose touch with how their properties are operating. You want to get all the skeletons out of the closet and uncover as many problems as possible. In some ways, purchasing an existing building can be like buying a used car. Some blemishes are visible, but some are not so apparent.

While due diligence is your homework assignment, you don't have to do it all by yourself. A good team of specialists (roofers, plumbers and electricians, among others) is needed to provide expertise on specific aspects of a property. A general contractor experienced in the type of property you are buying will be helpful as well. Some professionals might charge fees to do an inspection, but talk to your broker before shelling out cash. He or she might have relationships with people who will do the work as a favor in hope of getting your business in the future. You can also ask for bids for work that needs to be done on the property. Contractors will be happy to provide you with a bid at no cost.

Keep this in mind: No matter how well you do your homework, there often will be a few details about a property that are tough to detect. A client of mine once bought an office building and hired a heating, ventilation and air-conditioning expert to inspect the HVAC system. The inspector checked out the four rooftop units, and he deemed them to be in good working order. All else looked good, so my client bought the building that fall and moved in.

The next summer, he called me and said he couldn't get one part of the building to stay cool. The HVAC contractor came back out and took a more thorough look at the building. With this second inspection he determined that the building had an addition that wasn't readily apparent when he had first examined the building. The HVAC system from the original structure had been extended into the addition, but the ducts in the addition were too small to carry an adequate amount of air to that space. Another cooling unit had to be added to the building. As this example proves, buildings are unique creatures, and there are often a few surprises here and there.

While the physical inspection process is important, a working knowledge of functionality and market rents is equally crucial. Two industrial developers bought a large tract of land on a high-traffic arterial that was zoned for retail development. They subdivided the property into five lots and sold four of them. A movie theater, a furniture store, a bank and a restaurant were built on the four lots. The developers then decided to build a retail strip center on the remaining lot even though they had little retail development experience. They also apparently hired an architect who hadn't done much retail building design.

Not knowing the needs of retail tenants in the marketplace, the architect designed a building to make optimal use of the lot, and the developers broke ground on the structure before securing any tenants.

The building which they constructed was 100 feet deep, but the average retail tenant at that time only occupied 1,000 to 1,200 square feet of space. It didn't take them long to realize that the typical tenant couldn't operate a business in a space that was 10 to 12 feet wide and 100 feet deep. There were also not very many large retail tenants in the market at that time.

To make the financing work, the developers had

projected higher rents that were to be paid by smaller tenants. If they rented large spaces, the rent per square foot would be lower, and the developers would be required by the lender to put more cash into the project. They didn't have the cash, so they became creative in order to fill the space. To attract a larger tenant at above-market rents, they gave away as much as one year of rent on a five-year lease and made a personal loan to one tenant so the company could buy inventory for their store. Then, they divided the remaining space into some unique configurations that would be difficult to rent out a second time around.

With the building finally filled up, they sold it to an out-of-town investor based on the artificially high rental income. As the leases expired, most of the tenants couldn't afford the above-market rents and vacated the building. The new owners spent a lot of money reconfiguring the building and worked through lengthy vacancies only to fill the building with tenants at much lower rents. They then sold the building for a substantial loss. If the buyer had done their due diligence properly they would have recognized that the rents the tenants were paying were above market. They also might have figured out that, if the existing tenants moved out in the future, the odd-sized space might be hard to re-lease. Had they done their home work—their due diligence—up front, they could have saved a lot of time and money.

So, it is really important to do your homework and to consider the physical, financial, technical and practical aspects of a property. Here's a basic checklist that will help guide you through the due diligence process. Again, a knowledgeable broker can help you walk through the due diligence steps and he or she will have relationships with construction professionals who can assist you in the process.

Due Diligence Check List

Physical:
- ☐ Roof inspection
- ☐ Heating, ventilation and air-conditioning inspection
- ☐ Structural inspection
- ☐ Property condition report
- ☐ Asbestos study
- ☐ Environmental reports
- ☐ Electrical inspection
- ☐ Plumbing inspection
- ☐ Parking and landscaping condition

Financial:
- ☐ Current income and expense information
- ☐ Historical income and expense information
- ☐ Seller's federal income-tax reporting

Technical:
- ☐ Property zoning classification
- ☐ County Assessors tax notes
- ☐ Municipal sign regulations
- ☐ Preliminary title report and abstract information
- ☐ Building plans
- ☐ Service contracts affecting the premises

☐ Boundary line survey
☐ Traffic count map
☐ Current property appraisal
☐ Aerial photographs
☐ Leases and tenant information
☐ Energy audit
☐ Air quality report
☐ Building rules and regulations
☐ Parking code
☐ Flood zone

Practical:
☐ Does the property have adequate parking?
☐ Are the building's space configurations flexible?
☐ Is the building divisible?
☐ Are the rents at market prices?
☐ Are the expenses realistic?
☐ Is the building design timeless?
☐ What is the marketability of the property?
☐ Can the building accommodate a variety of
   tenants?
☐ Is the property well lit and safe at night?
☐ Does traffic have good access from all directions?

Once you have completed your due diligence you can determine if you are ready to move forward with the purchase of the property. If substantial, previously unknown or undisclosed issues have arisen during the due diligence process, you may need to go back to the seller and try to remedy those issues. The most common issues that I have encountered over the years are related to unexpected repairs and environmental issues. The seller thinks his roof is in satisfactory condition and the buyer gets an inspection and finds out that the roof really needs to be replaced at a cost of $20,000. Now what would you do? In fairness, most of the value of a new roof will accrue to you as the new owner of the property, but you tied up the building under the understanding that the roof was in good condition. So, you would do your best to negotiate what you think is a fair settlement, or you would pass and go on to another property.

Many years ago a partner and I had tied up a piece of land on which we planned to erect an office building. We completed our due diligence on the property and we were ready to remove our contingencies and proceed to closing. The listing information sheet on the property provided by the seller's broker clearly stated "city sewer is in the street in front of the property". This was one item we had not verified. At the last minute, my partner thought he should go down to the city and verify this information. It was a good thing he did, because he found out that in fact the sewer line ended 150 feet from our property in solid rock. As I recall, the estimate we obtained to extend the sewer to the property was about $25,000. That might not seem like much money today, but at the time it was a lot of money to us. We went back to the listing broker and let him know we were not happy about his negligence on the facts. I don't remember if he or the seller was at fault for providing the wrong information. We told the broker that in order to close, we would need a discount from the seller to cover this unexpected cost. The seller was very upset but finally agreed and gave us a discount on the price at closing in consideration of the error.

Not all sellers are going to remedy issues that arise

during your due diligence, but it is always worth a try to see if you can work something out.

It is not uncommon to go through due diligence on an older, run-down property and find out that the costs to get the building in good shape do not justify the price you have agreed to pay. Again, you try and renegotiate your deal or you pass and move on to other properties.

I could write a whole book on the due diligence process. There is a lot to know and cover. This chapter has mainly highlighted some of the physical aspects of due diligence. Another key part is your review of the financial aspects of the property. Here, a clear understanding of real estate math is essential. We'll dive into the math later in the book, but for now let's look at a paradox in the math of success: the value of losing.

Sometimes your best investments are
the ones you don't make.
                    Donald Trump

~ 12 ~
Lose To Learn

When asked about his failures at invention, Thomas A. Edison said that he had not failed at all. Rather, he said he had succeeded in finding hundreds of ways that would **not** work. He added that once he had eliminated ways that didn't work he would find one way that was successful.

When entering the world of real estate investing, you're likely to try some things that don't work. You aren't likely to try hundreds of them, as Edison did, but you will make mistakes along the way. There is a learning curve with any new endeavor—whether it's a new job, hobby or business venture—and real estate investing is no exception. You can read all of the books on the subject, and as I've said, there are some good ones. But the real-world lessons start when you put down the books and start investing on your own.

Real estate investing is a step-by-step process. With experience in the market, you gain additional insight into the ins and outs of each crucial step. You will make mistakes in the process, and you will do some things that you aren't likely to do again.

Does this mean you will lose money? Perhaps. In fact, it's likely you will lose money at some point in the learning process; it's almost a rite of passage in real estate. I have been fortunate over the years not to have lost a lot of money during the learning process, but I will never forget the times I did lose a few bucks.

Here is the most important advice I can give you on this topic. Face your challenges and deal with them. Do not stick your head in the sand and avoid the issues. That only makes things worse. Remember that making mistakes and losing money is a normal part of life and learning. I have seen many people freeze up or avoid their problems when they know they are going to take a loss. Being proactive when challenges arise is an essential skill you must acquire in life and in real estate investing. Life is not always just a walk in the park. If you avoid its challenges, you will never learn and grow; if you do not deal with challenges they tend to get worse and more costly.

In our current recession I have seen many quality people end up with tough real estate issues. The people who go to their lender and work hard to resolve things may end up losing money, but they gain peace of mind and are able to move on with their lives and on to future successes. You might wonder if there is a special process in these situations. The answer is, each property and related financing situation is different. The key is direct and active communication with your lender. If you have a complicated or contentious situation, a good real estate attorney may be required. Face the situation, deal with it, take your bumps and move on.

Upon learning those lessons, many people give up and go back to other forms of investing that appear to be less risky. As we've learned in recent years, however, all forms of investing carry risk. Those who stick with real estate and learn from their mistakes typically go on to reap the long-term rewards that come with successful real estate investing.

As you pass through these financial trials, you will move closer to a true understanding of what it takes to be a skillful real estate investor. Go into real estate investing knowing that you might have to lose to learn, and rest assured that this is a normal and expected part of the process.

I have learned over the years that no matter how good you get at real estate investing you will always have a few investments that do not turn out as well as you expected. The odds are, if you make ten real estate investments, it is likely that a couple of those properties will not perform up to your expectations. You may sell them and lose some money. Time does heal a lot of financial wounds with real estate, so you may just hang on to them and ride it out.

I have three parcels of land I purchased thirty years ago with some partners. At the time we thought the land would go up in value quickly and we would sell those properties and make a lot of money. That did not happen. So, here it is thirty years later, and the land has been paid-for for a long time. Some day we will sell the land and make a profit. Time will bring us a small return on the money we invested.

Now here is the good news: Out of ten properties you may purchase, there are bound to be a couple of "home run" properties. Sometimes things go better than you thought. Again, when you put time and real estate together, some interesting things can happen. I have had a couple of situations over the years where a neighbor really wanted or needed to purchase the property I owned next door to them. They paid top dollar and I made some excellent returns on my investment. So, if you buy right, the balance of the ten properties you purchase may turn out to be good, solid performers.

One example where a neighbor really wanted a property my partners and I owned was a piece of land we purchased many years ago on which to build a couple of office buildings. The land was on a main arterial street with a middle school behind it. All of the land fronting the street was zoned for office development, and the school athletic grounds were behind all of the properties on this block. Most of the lots fronting the street still had single family homes on them.

We purchased the property on the corner of the arterial and a side street that provided access to the school. There was a single family home on the property we purchased, and we leased the home out for $450 per month. That rent made our payment on part of the purchase price financed by the seller. The home west of us was occupied by a home owner. On the other side of the home owner, there were two homes owned by a developer friend of mine by the name of Bob. He also planned to develop his property but had the two homes rented out until he was ready to move forward with development. Bob had purchased his property ten years before we purchased our parcel and had paid $1 per square foot for it. That had been a good value at the time for an office building site. When we purchased our property ten years later, the economy had dipped and we were able to purchase our property for $1 per square foot as well. In my mind that was a great buy, especially with the income from the house to make our payment until we developed the property.

After we'd held the property for a few years the school approached us as well as all of the property owners along the strip, and advised us that they needed our land for expansion of the school. This was many years ago so I do not recall the exact sales price, but I know that after a lengthy negotiation the school paid us $3.65 per square foot. So, in a few short years we ended up with a very nice return on our investment. That property was one of the ten that became winners.

As I think about it, almost all of my mentors have had a few really challenging properties or ones they lost money on during their investing careers. No matter how smart or experienced you are, it is impossible to be exactly right 100% of the time.

With that in mind, consider starting small. I have watched a lot of people jump into real estate investing with big money on their first investment and lose a big chunk during the learning curve. Start small with manageable amounts of debt, and it won't be as painful if you do lose money. Regardless of how that first property performs financially, you'll be that much closer to cresting the learning curve—and that much closer to long-term success in real estate investing. So stick with it and keep investing, even after you have had a few challenging investment experiences.

Now, if you thought it was ironic that one could find success by "Losing to Learn", prepare yourself for the next paradox in real estate investing: You have to spend money to make money!

*Doing little things well is a step
toward doing big things better.*

Harry F. Banks

~ 13 ~
You Make Your Money When You Buy!

Ellis Levitt, the second-generation leader of Dial Finance (now Wells Fargo Financial), learned a valuable lesson when he sat down at his first real estate negotiation. The well-organized young Levitt gave a solid presentation to the shrewd, elderly Frederick M. Hubbell. In his exuberance, he said, "You have to admit, Mr. Hubbell that it's worth what we're asking for it."

Hubbell replied, "Any damned fool with money can buy something for what it's worth."

That was in 1914, but the lesson Levitt learned nearly 100 years ago is still true today: Anybody with money can buy—or finance—something for what it's worth. I read the above story in the Des Moines Register when I was growing up in Iowa and it has stuck with me.

I am a value investor. I am always looking for a bargain—or for a property from which more value can be created. The reason is simple: I make my money when I buy. And if you are careful and disciplined, you will make money when you buy too. No, you won't have profits in hand when you purchase, but the decisions you make and the terms you agree to will play a big part in how much money you will make in the future.

Consequently, the key in real estate investing is always to make a good buy. That means simply this: Buy a property for less than it's worth (or could be worth if certain steps are taken to increase its value).

How do you go about making sure you are getting a good buy? The best offense can be a good defense. If you are looking to purchase an income property, the first thing you need is real numbers—real income and real expenses. That might require you to dig deeper than the information provided by the seller or his broker. Sure, there are some sellers out there who have complete, professional sales packages. That said, most real estate brokers and owners will provide you with less information than you need to make an informed decision. You will need to play Sherlock Holmes and review all of the information you are given, making sure you have all of the actual, current facts and figures.

The key word in the last sentence is *current.* I have received many rent rolls that look good on paper, only to learn that one or more of the tenants listed no longer leased space in the building, or they were in the process of moving out.

When looking at rents, look for properties that have below-market rents. If you buy a building with below-market rents, you'll likely be able to raise rents and increase the value of the property.

While you must examine the rent rolls closely, don't shy away completely from vacant buildings if you have the financial capacity to make monthly payments until you find a tenant. Also, if you have some money to put toward minor improvements don't be afraid to buy a building that has a little hair on it, as I like to say. A building with a little hair on it can look pretty sharp and much more rentable if you give it a shave, or clean it up a little bit. With this perspective, you will see opportunities where others see problems.

When looking at a potential property, remember to exercise due diligence on the expense side of the equation. It can be just as incomplete—and potentially harmful to your bottom line—as inaccurate income information. Make sure you are aware of all current and anticipated expenses affecting the property, including future capital expenses such as roofs, HVAC units and parking lot repairs.

Of course, in addition, you will need to have—or gain quickly—a good grasp of the overall market and how the property in question compares to other properties on the market. Determine what you are willing to pay for a specific type of property in your market. Make offers until you find a seller who is motivated enough to accept your offer.

If you aren't in a rush and look long enough, you will eventually make an offer that's accepted and get a good deal. It might take a lot of time, but patience and persistence is what separates the successful investor from those who wonder how you got such a great deal. If you stay with it long enough and have the knowledge to recognize a good deal when it comes across your desk, you will be successful.

One key ingredient for a good buy is a motivated seller. Look for the type of properties you want and situations where you have someone who really wants to sell. There are all kinds of reasons that a seller may be motivated to sell at what is a good price to you. Keep in mind that they are not always driven just by the price they get out of a property. I can think of a seller we represented that was a very financially strong and astute

real estate owner. Their business objective was to get rid
of the property at whatever price it took to get it sold and
move on to other more pressing business issues they had.
They gladly sold the property at what a buyer thought
was a good buy and were glad to do so. As the saying goes,
"One man's trash is another man's treasure."

One word of advice: If you want to make a good buy on
a promising property, be realistic. There are people who
are so unrealistic with their lowball offers that they make
a lot of offers and never buy anything. There is nothing
wrong with coming in low, but if you want to get into the
game, you have to be realistic about what it's going
to take.

When many people think about investing in real
estate, they envision buying a building. Buildings can be
good purchases, but the best bargains and the most
potential for opportunity I have found has been in buying
land. Since commercial land doesn't generate income, it
isn't as liquid as other types of real estate. Therefore,
when people have to sell in a hurry, they typically must
take what they can get from the relatively small pool of
buyers who have the financial capacity to buy land.

Investing in land isn't for everybody. It takes a lot of
financial resources, a high tolerance for risk, and
knowledge in the arena of developing land to make a
profit. Land buyers must consider how long they will have
to hold the property to get it developed and factor in what
improvements the land needs to be resold at a profit.
Land buyers must have the financial wherewithal to
make a down payment and to make the monthly
payments necessary to carry the property until it can be

developed or resold.

Here's an example: An individual inherits land and is desperate to unload it either because he needs the money or the annual real estate taxes are a burden—often, those factors go hand in hand. Let's say that after some negotiation, you agree to buy the land for $250,000 with a down payment of $50,000. The seller agrees to carry the balance of $200,000 on a promissory note and deed of trust, with interest, for a monthly payment of $2,000. The success of such a transaction relies on your ability to make the $2,000-per-month payments while you are working on a plan to develop or resell the property.

Many people don't have the ability to take on this type of investment. For those who do have the financial capacity and a vision for how the property can be developed or improved, profits can be incredible.

Years ago, I sold a property like this to an investor who then subdivided the land into four lots. By the time he had successfully completed the subdivision, the best of the four lots was worth what he paid for the entire property. The sale of the other three lots proved to be his profit. In another case, the rezoning of a piece of property from residential to commercial tripled its value.

And finally, some people simply find awesome development opportunities. What's an awesome opportunity? Let's say you bought the last piece of land in a quickly developing retail area that had all of the typical neighborhood services except a tire store. You now might be in a position to go to a tire store and offer to build and lease them a building. That's a great opportunity for them—and for you.

Of all the real estate investments I've made, the

greatest returns I have enjoyed came from well-located properties that were bought and somehow enhanced by subdividing, rezoning or some other development opportunity.

These examples aren't exceptions to a rule; these kinds of opportunities are available to those who search hard and buy smart. There is always a bargain out there somewhere, but it won't have a big sign on it that says, "Bargain Real Estate Deal." You need to put in the time and effort and have the market knowledge to realize when you're in a position to make money when you buy.

Any damned fool with money can buy
something for what it is worth.
                                Frederick M. Hubbell

~ 14 ~
Common Investing Mistakes

There are three basic ways people get themselves into trouble with real estate investments:

1. *They pay too much.*
2. *They borrow too much.*
3. *They don't do much homework.*

In other words, they get *muched.*

The successful real estate investors I know believe you make your money when you buy, which is contrary to the school of thought employed by a lot of real estate speculators. Many bet that a property is going to go up in value, so they are more focused on getting in on easy terms and sometimes they pay less attention to the fundamentals, making the assumption their investment's value will increase. They just want to ride the market on its way up, and then get out.

The reality is this: A lot of money is lost and made in the ups and downs of the real estate cycle, and it's impossible to time the market to maximize profits every time. What we've seen happen during the real estate market bust in recent years is a prime example. Many investors leveraged themselves to the max assuming that real estate values would continue to increase. After a number of years of this kind of investing, the greater-fool theory came into play. "*If I buy now,*" speculators thought, "*values are going to go up. Someone is going to pay a big price for my property, and I'll make a lot of money and get out of the market.*"

As we have found out, that theory only works for so long. Ever play the game "Catch Phrase"? The game involves two teams and a small disk which holds a card with many words on it. A single word appears through a small window on the disk's surface. Each team captain takes turns holding the device and giving clues to his teammates in hopes that they can guess the word on the disk. Once the team guesses correctly, the team captain passes the device to the captain of the opposing team, who gets a new word. During the time the teams are trying to guess the words on the disk, a timer sounds off randomly, increasing in frequency as time passes until a buzzer rings to signal the end of the round. The team holding the disk and still trying to guess the word when the buzzer rings loses that round of the game.

Speculative commercial real estate investing is similar, as the one who is stuck with the property when the proverbial buzzer goes off and prices decline is the loser.

One of my friends has a very simple solution. He only buys properties for 80% or less of what he thinks they are worth. His goal is to create value and margin every time he buys. If he is negotiating a purchase and can't get to a number that meets his goals, he moves on. He'll continue looking and making offers until he finds something that fits his objectives. You make your money when you buy, so learn how to buy right.

The next mistake is borrowing too much. Leverage is a

wonderful component of real estate investing, but too much leverage can get an investor into big trouble.

Through the years, I have seen many good people lose everything because they borrowed too much money to buy real estate. Here's what happens. They buy a few pieces of property and get the process down. After a couple of successes, they begin to get a little too confident and start to borrow against the properties they have purchased to buy more properties. They also try the super-leverage ideas they have read about in get-rich-quick real estate books. In a relatively short period of time, they amass a sizeable portfolio of properties with very little equity and a massive amount of debt. Invariably, something tips them over. The real estate cycle swings in the wrong direction or they lose a few key tenants. Then, the resulting negative cash flow quickly devours their finances.

Be prudent in your borrowing. After the financial challenges our country has experienced in recent years, I'm inclined to move forward with extreme caution and be debt averse. When taking on development projects in the future, I don't plan on borrowing more than 60% of the money required to complete those projects. I would rather have more partners, a smaller percentage of ownership and a smaller amount of risk. Don't borrow too much.

The third common mistake is that investors don't do enough homework. Consequently, they encounter problems with the property that will affect its financial performance during the time they own it. Ultimately, that means they pay too much.

Through the years, a number of real estate investors

have come to me for help after they bought a property. Oftentimes, they have a mess on their hands because they made one—or more—of these common mistakes: paid too much for the property, borrowed too much money to buy the property, or didn't do their homework adequately before closing on the deal. If only these investors had come to me before signing on the dotted line!

I'll give you an example of a couple that came to me after the damage was done. They made only one of these mistakes—they didn't do their homework—but it still gave them financial headaches for years.

The couple had invested in rental homes and duplexes through the years and had been quite successful doing so. However, they were tired of dealing with residential tenants, and thought it would be easier to manage one commercial property. They decided they were ready to move up and invest in a commercial building.

Working with the real estate broker who had helped them with their residential investments, they looked at a few buildings and agreed to make an offer on a three-tenant commercial building on a busy arterial street.

The listing broker represented the property as fully leased. The couple reviewed the income-and-expense projections provided by that broker. The numbers suggested the property's income would cover the mortgage payment and provide them with some decent cash flow.

They struck a deal that was well-crafted and quite creative. The couple would trade their residential rental properties for the three-tenant commercial building. The commercial building was worth $325,000 and had a $225,000 loan in place which the couple would take over.

The commercial building owner would take the couple's residential rental properties that had no debt. After accounting for commissions and closing costs, the equities on each side of the transaction were evenly matched and the trade was fair for both parties. The only challenge was that there was no cash generated to pay closing costs and commissions. To cover the real estate broker's commissions and closing costs, a mortgage was created on one of the rental properties and sold at a discount to generate cash. Everyone seemed pleased with the arrangement, and the transaction closed soon thereafter.

Within a couple of months, however, the proverbial honeymoon was over. The couple was unsuccessful in their attempt to collect rent from one of the tenants, only to find out the tenant hadn't been paying rent for three to four months prior to closing. They started eviction proceedings. At about the same time, another tenant that they thought was on a long-term lease gave notice and moved out of the building.

Shortly thereafter, the couple called me and asked for help. Unfortunately, there wasn't anything I could do for them at that stage, aside from marketing the empty space. The income from the third and only remaining tenant didn't cover the mortgage payment and the monthly operating expenses of the building. This put the couple in a financial position that they had not anticipated.

At this point, it became apparent that they hadn't received good guidance from their real estate broker. No one had read the leases closely or investigated the tenant's credit or payment history.

This is the kind of transaction that can turn into a lawsuit. I don't recall whether this one ended up in court, but it was a mess. It could easily have been avoided if the couple and their broker had done their homework.

A normal part of due diligence should have been to request a copy of the leases and closely review them in detail. What was the length of each lease? How much rent was being paid by each tenant? Who paid what expenses? Were there options to extend the leases? Credit checks should have been done on the tenants. Talking with each tenant may have given the couple some indication of the tenant's level of business success or lack thereof. The buyers could have requested a rental payment history on the tenants from the sellers. More work should have been done by the buyers during the due diligence period. Let's look at how to avoid mistakes like this in the next chapter!

In the chapters on prudent process, due diligence and common mistakes, you saw example after example of what happens when an investor doesn't do their homework. You must become an expert in the functional attributes of the type of property you want to buy, contract clauses and governmental issues.

One functional issue—and there are many—is the size of the spaces in a building. If most tenants in the marketplace want 20-foot-by-60-foot bays, and the building you're looking to buy has 20-foot-by-80-foot bays, this could present an issue.

When it comes to contracts, it is vitally important that you understand lease clauses and how they determine what costs the tenants bear and what costs the building owner incurs. During one winter of record snowfall in

Spokane, many building owners, including myself, paid to have the snow shoveled off their roofs so that the roofs wouldn't collapse under the unprecedented snow load. One of my partners owns a large building, and the bill for shoveling the roof came in at more than $20,000. As he reviewed the leases, it became apparent the documents were written in such a manner that he couldn't pass this cost on to the tenants. Needless to say, it's important to be able to understand the financial ramifications of the leases in place in a building before you buy it.

Finally, we have governmental issues. Frequently, these have to do with land-use zoning, which can severely limit a property's uses. If the potential uses for a property are limited because of zoning laws, it could take longer to get space leased out when it becomes vacant. Also, many cities' sign laws are becoming stricter, while some tenants want maximum exposure to passing traffic. If that exposure is curtailed because of sign regulations, they might seek another property.

As you can see, not doing enough homework frequently leads to several investment mistakes like paying too much for a property and borrowing too much money. It can become a cycle of missteps that leads to headaches and financial heartache. The good news is that these mistakes can be avoided with a little prudence and a lot of hard work. So remember, don't get *muched!*

By failing to prepare, you are preparing to fail.
Ben Franklin

~ Notes ~

~ 15 ~
Finding a Bargain:
How to Make Pigs Fly

Finding a bargain isn't just a good way to go when looking for investment real estate; it's the best way to go if you want to build equity quickly and create the potential for strong cash flow over a long period.

Keep in mind, however, one important point about real estate: What might be a bargain for you as the buyer is likely a bane for the seller. The transaction can be a win-win if the seller gets rid of his headache—and if you can create value out of your investment. But you need to find out quickly why the seller has the property priced below market value, and you need to determine what, precisely, the seller wants or needs to get out of the transaction.

The seller simply might need cash, and you just might be the one who comes along with the cash at the right time. Or, the owner might be carrying too much debt on the property. The building might have a long-standing vacancy. Or, the property might need a large investment of capital, either for needed improvements, style updates or environmental cleanup.

In some cases, the property has some sort of defect or problem the seller simply doesn't want to address or hasn't figured out how to fix. If you can either figure out a solution to the problem or a way to deal with the defect, you can create value that wasn't there before, hence the bargain.

Just because a property appears to be a bargain does not necessarily mean it's going to be a good investment. About thirty years ago, my partners and I purchased a number of land parcels that were really inexpensive. At the time they each seemed like a great bargain. However, the development and growth that we expected to take place around those properties didn't happen. Fortunately, we paid off the loans we used to purchase those properties a long time ago, so we own the land free and clear. But we still have to pay the taxes and the upkeep on the properties each year. Development is now starting to take place near those properties, so maybe in the next thirty years we will be able to sell the land and get a return on our investment. Land investments can carry a much higher degree of risk, and this would be one example of that.

It takes in-depth market knowledge and a lot of looking to find what might be a bargain. Then it takes making a lot of offers and weeding out properties that turn out to be of less quality than they appear. Prospective properties don't have a big sign on them saying, "Bargain Real Estate Investment! Buy Me Now!" Many bargains are "created" by smart investors with a mindset that says things like, "*Find me a pig and let's see if we can put some lipstick on it and make it fly.*"

One bargain that fits this description is a single tenant office building that was offered for sale as an investment a few years ago. The building was well built and in a good location. The down side was that the existing tenant had only 18 months left on their lease and they had told the owners that they were not interested in extending the lease. So, many investors looked at the property but they were all put off by the short term lease. The building sat on the market for six months and no offers were made on it. By this time the owners were getting increasingly motivated to sell and stated that they would consider taking less than the asking price to get the property sold. A smart investor made them a low offer subject to inspecting the condition of the property and obtaining financing. The sellers accepted his offer. Then guess what the investor did? He went to the tenant, and through a creative proposal he got the tenant to agree to a new five year lease! That turned his purchase into a great bargain. Here was a property that everyone knew about but it took a creative investor to figure out how to turn it into a great investment. That pig did fly!

Through the years, most of the good deals I've found and purchased are properties like the one above that had sat on the market for a long time. I watched and studied those properties until it seemed like the timing was right to make an offer. I also had a plan for how to make the property a good investment if I was able to buy it at the right price.

One example is an old 5,000 square foot cinderblock building across the street from the church my wife and I attend. The building was originally a grocery store in the 1930s, and through the years, it had housed a number of different businesses. At the time the building went on the market, the owner was using it to operate a dry cleaning business.

The property had been for sale for well over a year,

and it had many drawbacks. The building essentially covered the entire lot, and the only available parking was on the street. It was a disaster on the inside, and it needed an environmental cleanup due to the dry cleaning solvents used on the premises. The condition of the property and the unknown environmental cleanup costs had sent all potential buyers running.

I observed the property each Sunday as we attended church and I watched as the asking price was repeatedly reduced. The location was excellent, and there really was plenty of parking on the street. I had a friend who did environmental cleanup, and I knew I could at least tie down the cost to get it cleaned.

When my wife mentioned that a friend needed a new location for her beauty shop, I thought I might have a potential tenant for the building and offered the owner $125,000 for the property. The asking price at that time had been lowered to $155,000, and after lengthy negotiations, we settled at $132,000. I had contingencies written into the deal regarding the environmental cleanup to ensure I wasn't getting myself into something that would take years and a lot of money to remedy. The environmental cleanup costs did come in higher than I expected—at about $7,500—and the seller and I agreed to split those costs. Getting all the environmental issues resolved with the Washington State Department of Ecology took some time, but it was doable.

Unfortunately, during this rather lengthy process, the beauty salon owner found another location. However, around the same time, a colleague of mine who is a broker mentioned that he had a client who was looking for about 5,000 square feet of space for records storage. I suggested this building to him, and he said it sounded like a good fit. My friend also asked if, with his client's approval, he could buy into the building with me. I agreed, and we finished the environmental cleanup and closed on the purchase of the property. We both agreed that we would purchase the property even if his tenant did not move forward with a lease.

The cleanup project was immense. My son and a friend started clearing out the junk left in the building from the dry cleaning business. They ended up taking 22 pickup loads to the dump. After that, I hired a demolition contractor to dismantle the mammoth dry cleaning equipment at the back of the building. The contractor disassembled what he could, but some larger parts had to be cut up with an acetylene torch so that they could be removed with a forklift. Dismantling that equipment cost about $5,000. Most prospective purchasers would have taken one look at the large dry cleaning machinery and said, "Forget it." We pressed on, however, scrubbing the walls and giving the inside a fresh coat of white paint.

My partner gave his client a tour of the building, and the client said it was exactly what they needed. It was close to the company's main facility, and at $1,850 per month, the rent was reasonable considering the prime location and the amount of space. Since the building was being used for storage, parking wasn't an issue.

With the improvements and the new lease, the value of the building was high enough that we were able to borrow money to cover the cost of the building and all of the improvements. We discuss later in this book the pitfalls of **no-down financing** (see Chapter 20), but in this instance, we were able to secure a building in a great location with a credit tenant on a long-term lease, without any money out of our pockets. So in this unique instance, the no-down option carried with it a relatively low level of risk.

In the end, we acquired a good building in a great location and figured out how to remedy the problems at a reasonable cost. Bargains are out there if you know how to solve the problems that are often an inherent part of real estate ownership. You just have to do your homework, know what you are willing to take on, and have a vision for the upside. You know, the "flying pig."

We simply attempt to be fearful when others are greedy and to be greedy only when others are fearful.
Warren Buffett

~ 16 ~
Accumulation

Detractors say one of the shortcomings of investing in real estate is that it doesn't have liquidity. In other words, you can't get your equity out quickly like you can with stocks or bonds. What others see as a drawback, however, I see as a distinct and amazing benefit. This lack of liquidity encourages investors to become good accumulators of assets. As far as I'm concerned, this is a key secret to investing success. Accumulation is the number one ingredient to building net worth. Let me repeat that: **Accumulation is the number one ingredient in building net worth.**

When my wife Kae and I were first married, we learned about the long-term benefits of making regular monthly investments into a mutual fund. We learned that if we invested just $25 per month in a mutual fund with an annual average return of 12%, we would have $500,000 by the time we were 65 years old. After reviewing a number of mutual funds, we chose Templeton's growth fund and began investing $25 per month. After a year or so, we raised our monthly investment to $50 a month.

In the first 3-1/2 years of our marriage, we made a few extra contributions, and our mutual fund increased in value. Before we knew it the combination of our contributions and the increase in the value of the fund resulted in a total value of in value to $2,800! In 1975, this was a lot of money for a young married couple. What did we do? We pulled the money out of the investment and bought a newer model car. What would have grown to become a half-million bucks became a four-wheeled depreciating asset.

As a young couple, we had not developed the maturity or the discipline to stay the course with our monthly investment program. We couldn't resist the allure of a newer car, and the money we had invested was just too easy to access.

You don't develop a large net worth by selling your assets and spending the proceeds. You develop net worth through the simple act of disciplined accumulation. This is not rocket science, but it is a discipline that many of us have a hard time cultivating. It doesn't come naturally for most; it takes time and effort to figure it out.

In the past couple of decades, our country has been focused on excess spending and consumption, which resulted in the financial mess we are currently experiencing. People have also been borrowing too much and saving too little. This trend may have slowed for a little while, but it took an abrupt change in the economy for most people to re-evaluate their spending habits and to start saving more.

Over time, I have developed a buy-and-hold philosophy with real estate, but there have been times I've had to deviate from my plan. Sometimes things don't go as anticipated. A property might have some characteristic that makes it less than a stellar performer, and it might be best to sell and move on. Or, someone offers you more money than the property is worth, and you sell and invest those proceeds in another property.

One thing to keep in mind about selling investment real estate: You will pay capital gains taxes on the sale unless you do a **tax-deferred exchange**. As a result of these taxes, selling can actually reduce your net worth.

When you own real estate, you are less inclined to hastily sell a piece of property to satisfy a material desire. It takes time to put a property on the market and get it sold. This lack of quick liquidity is actually a great benefit. It usually does not allow us to make quick impulse decisions with our real estate investments

I sometimes wonder what would have happened if Kae and I had used those mutual-fund dollars to buy a rental home. I'm sure it would have been a different story. We would have had to go through the process of selling the home, which would have taken time. That time might have caused us to rethink our priorities for those funds and have the discipline to stick to our original plan to save for the future.

Not to diverge from the main topic, but Kae and I eventually restarted our regular monthly mutual fund investing program and have added more mutual funds to our portfolio through the years. We have learned to become much more disciplined accumulators. While my main expertise lies in real estate, I'm a firm believer in a diversified investment portfolio. Some mutual funds in addition to real estate provide part of that diversification.

So, no matter what type of investments you make, learn to become a successful accumulator. I am confident that the lack of liquidity in real estate investing helps many investors to become effective accumulators, which is a simple yet principal key to building wealth.

Wealth is accumulated by the acquisition of assets not the disposition of assets.

Jeff K. Johnson

~ 17 ~
Duplication

When I was a young commercial real estate broker just getting started in the business, I listed a small retail building for lease that had been occupied by Winchell's Donuts. Winchell's had closed the store and they hired me to find a tenant to take over the balance of their lease. Shortly after I listed the property, I got a call from a man who said he was interested in looking at the building.

I met him at the property and asked what his plans were for the building. He said that he and his wife had just purchased a new sandwich franchise and they were looking for their first location. The man was a former University of Idaho professor and he and his wife were selling some residential rental properties to fund this new business venture. He told me the new franchise was called Subway, that it had very low start up costs, and that he and his wife were expecting to make $30,000 per year from the store.

This was in the early 1980s and at that time, $30,000 was a reasonable profit to make from a small sandwich shop. I remember thinking, however, that this business was going to be a lot of work and risk for $30,000 per year. The couple would have the responsibility of managing employees and would need to oversee the shop seven days a week. At the time, I thought that their rental properties seemed like a better investment.

We negotiated a lease with Winchell's and the Subway farnchisee opened for business. The sandwich shop appeared to be doing well, but it soon became evident that it was not the right fit for them. So after a couple of years, they sold it to another franchisee. Over time, I watched as more and more Subway sandwich shops opened in Spokane. When the tally had reached about ten Subways, I did the math: Ten Subway shops making $30,000 per year added up to $300,000!

The real secret to making money with a Subway franchise was **duplication**: getting the business concept down and then repeating it! The same is true with real estate investing. You master the process then duplicate it. This is what most real estate investors I know have done to become successful. They start with one rental home and over time, they continue to duplicate the process and before you know it they have forty properties. Or, they start with one apartment building and eventually end up with ten large apartment complexes. Once you unlock the secrets of real estate investing, you just continue to apply what you have learned and duplicate the process. This is a simple concept, but it does take time, effort and motivation to keep going through the steps. The outcome can be very rewarding. And yes, you can probably make a lot of money in the restaurant business, but I personally think investing in real estate is a lot simpler.

I share this Subway story because almost everyone can visualize it. Most people have had a Subway sandwich and can picture one or multiple Subway stores near where they live. Envisioning multiple real estate investments, on the other hand, is not as easy to grasp.

Think about purchasing a number of properties over a period of time, working hard to keep them rented, and maintaining them in top condition. As you generate cash flow from your properties you must have the discipline to take that cash flow and make additional principal payments on your mortgages. Then one day you make that final payment and one of your mortgages is paid off! With no mortgage payment, your cash flow increases and you can begin to pay off other mortgages! The whole process begins to snowball, allowing you to pay off more and more mortgages.

I can remember the first property I paid off. My partners and I had not taken any cash flow out of this property in the fifteen years we had owned it. I have to admit, the property was not a stellar performer, but we did make extra principal payments with the little cash flow we generated. Finally, we made the last payment on the mortgage and the building was paid for. At that point the property produced cash flow that resulted in each of us collecting a check for about $300 per month. That might not sound like a lot of money today, but that property produced cash flow that would actually grow with inflation over the years.

The next property we paid off resulted in checks for $500 per month for each of us. Over time, after duplicating our efforts and purchasing multiple properties, those monthly checks started adding up to real money! Remember the ten Subway sandwich shops generating $30,000 each per year? How about ten paid-for homes or buildings, each generating $500 per month and totaling $60,000 per year? We are talking entry-level dollars here. You can see the power of this principle.

I am amazed at how simple some of the key real estate investing principles are, but they need to be put into action! Duplication is one of the simple but key secrets to real estate investing. Once you figure out a real estate investing formula that works for you, continue to duplicate it. Start small and work your way up one property at a time. Just keep duplicating your successes!

Big shots are only little shots who keep shooting.
Christopher Morley

~ 18 ~
Single Family Homes

Many successful real estate investors I know got started in the business by investing in single-family homes. Some of them built great wealth with single family homes but most of them eventually moved on to multifamily or commercial properties. Investing in single family homes still remains one of the easiest ways to get into real estate investing and to learn the basics of the business. On the other hand, it can also be labeled as *The Real Estate Investing School of Hard Knocks*. Investing in single family homes is hard work and requires special expertise and assertiveness.

Most single family home investors I know run their investments as a small family business with all family members helping out. The parents handle the acquisition and renting of the homes and their children assist with the day to day maintenance chores. This is an invaluable educational opportunity for those kids: It is a great way to invest for their college education and provide them unique work experience, and they can be part of the family enterprise.

When I got started in my real estate career in the Midwest in 1975, my mentor, Frank Takes was such an investor. Frank's wife Mary Lou assisted with the business, and their children helped out as soon as they were old enough to do so. Frank and many of his family members are still active real estate investors today.

At that time in the 1970s, Frank's goal was to find and buy homes for $12,000 to $20,000, and fix them up to rent and sell for a profit. Once, I found Frank a run-down home on a small lot that he was able to purchase from an estate for $3,500. In those days and at those prices, the math worked very well. With a few dollars in improvements, the homes could be rented for enough money to cover the mortgage payment and all of the expenses with cash flow left over. Frank spent several years fixing up and renting single family homes. He eventually sold many of them at a profit which enabled him to move into other types of real estate investments. I was fortunate to watch him build his real estate investing career using single family home purchases as a solid foundation.

With the drop in home prices across the United States in the last few years, single-family homes make sense once again as an investment. Prices reminiscent of the old days can now be found in a number of severely depressed, major housing markets around the country. A friend of mine and her husband recently bought four repossessed, newly constructed homes in Phoenix from a bank for only $40,000 each. If they can find tenants in that market— and sooner or later, they will be able to do so—that's a screaming deal.

For most beginners, the risk associated with purchasing one single-family home is manageable, and the startup costs can be saved in a relatively short period of time. Financing is a bit tougher to obtain than in the past, but you can still finance non-owner occupied, single family homes. If you have good credit, lenders will make loans on single family rental homes with 20% as a down payment.

In Spokane today, you can purchase a nice two-bedroom rental home for $60,000 to $75,000. That home will rent for $850 per month. With 20% down, a 25-year amortization and an interest rate of 6%, your payment will be between $600 and $700 per month. So, if you are careful you should be able to get the rent to cover the loan payment, real estate taxes, insurance and maintenance. You might even have some cash flow. My experience is that good economics, as it relates to single family home investments, is to put 20% down and have the rent cover all your costs. The majority of your return will come from appreciation over time and paying off the mortgage. If you are fortunate to buy really right you will create equity when you buy on the front end. As an example, let's say you find a highly motivated seller and you can purchase a home that could easily be worth $100,000 for $70,000. Maybe the home just needs $5,000 worth of clean up, paint and carpet to get back to its full value. That is a good buy. You can also create equity by purchasing homes that are in really poor repair and fixing them up.

Keep in mind that there is also the option of purchasing homes with seller financing. Seller financing was very popular back in the 70s when I was helping Frank find homes. Most of the homes Frank purchased were with seller financing and only 10% down. With seller financing you make a down payment to the seller and he carries a note and deed of trust for the balance owed. Payments are usually made to an escrow company which keeps track of the principal and interest paid for both parties until the loan is paid off. The escrow company holds the deed to the property and records the deed when the obligations of the contract have been met.

So the goal is to get into a home for a reasonable down payment and use the rental income to cover all of the expenses and your mortgage payment. If you buy right, you may end up with cash flow early on. As I mentioned above, your return comes mainly through appreciation and principle reduction. Your mortgage payment is fixed; as the years pass and rents increase with inflation, so should your cash flow.

One key ingredient to making money with rental homes is to choose your tenants as carefully as you select your properties. You are better off to wait for the right tenant than to be in a hurry and take a less-than-creditworthy tenant. Good tenants are worth their weight in gold and problem tenants can be very expensive.

The process of evicting a tenant can be time consuming and costly, especially if the tenant does not move out of your house. It is also not uncommon for an evicted or disgruntled tenant to trash your house and cost you thousands of dollars in repairs. I have heard of some landlords who actually agreed to pay tenants money if and after they move out of the house, just to get rid of them. So choosing the right people as renters is essential.

But if you choose your properties and your tenants wisely, you may be handsomely rewarded. An investor I know in Spokane accumulated 40 homes over a period of about twenty years and paid off the mortgages on all of them. He kept the homes rented and in good condition, and they provided him with a handsome retirement income. At the top of the market a few years ago, he was ready to retire from managing the homes and sold them for about $4.5 million. His years of hard work were well compensated.

I learned early in my career that I was too nice a guy to own residential rental property. If tenants were late with their rent, I typically fell for their sob stories and cut them slack. I would take them to the grocery store if they didn't have a car. I even made arrangements for a tenant with a bad cocaine habit to go into drug rehabilitation.

Compared with residential renters, I have found that the typical business tenant is much easier to deal with. Businesses do fall behind in rent, go broke, and move out in the middle of the night on occasion. In general, though, a businessperson's livelihood relies on having a place to work, and it's in his or her best interest to pay rent on time. Also, many residential tenants are in that market because they do not have the credit or the financial wherewithal to buy a home. This does not mean that there are not plenty of good creditworthy residential tenants. It is just important to make sure that they are the ones you choose to rent your properties.

If you do not have the personality to deal with residential tenants, there are property managers who specialize in managing single-family home investments. It is not, however, the most cost effective way to approach the business. The larger the properties you have, the more economies of scale you get. Again, the way most single family home investors make the most money is by doing most, if not all of the day-to-day maintenance work themselves. It becomes very expensive to hire a property manager and pay for someone to do all the repairs on your properties.

With most commercial properties, you can cost

effectively afford to hire a professional property manager to tend to the building and deal with tenants on your behalf. The same is true for larger apartment buildings as well. With any multifamily property consisting of 24 units or more, an investor can typically justify hiring a professional property management company to deal with tenants and handle the management details.

As we talked about in Chapter 7 on financial capacity, if the tenant moves out of your single family home, you need to be in a position to make the mortgage payment until you get a new tenant.

Plenty of real estate investors have gotten started in single-family homes. Do your homework and it can be a great way to get started in the business.

I have always felt secure and very safe with real estate. Real estate always appreciates.
Ivana Trump

~ 19 ~
Where Do I Get The Best Returns?

What types of real estate investments produce the best returns? Office buildings? Apartments? Warehouses? Retail buildings?

The simple answer is, all of the above. It is possible to make a good return on your investment with any kind of real estate. The key is to find the type of property that is best suited to your personality and investment style, then become an expert in what it takes to make money in that type of real estate.

All types of real estate have their own benefits and potential challenges. Let's look at some unique character-istics of the different types of investment real estate.

Retail properties can provide some incredible returns, but they typically have a higher cost of entry than other types of properties. Single tenant retail properties are one option to consider. These are buildings that are leased to just one tenant. There are single tenant retail properties in a wide range of prices and carry the advantage of long term leases to tenants who are local, regional or national. Many tenants occupying a single tenant retail property will sign a 10-year lease or longer. A long term lease is attractive to many investors, assuming that they have a tenant with good credit.

Here is an example: I recently received the offering of

a single tenant retail property for sale in Chicago. The building was newly constructed and leased to a national restaurant chain with good credit on a 20-year lease.

The property was offered for sale for $1,344,000 at a 9% cap rate. There are many properties of this type offered for sale all over the United States. The credit of the tenant varies as well as the quality of the location of the property. With today's financing you would likely need to come up with a down payment of 25% or about $336,000 to purchase this property. In addition you would need to have the financial capacity to make the mortgage payments if for any reason the tenant defaulted on their lease. So in this example, if you put $336,000 down and borrowed $1,008,000 at 6% interest with a 25-year amortization, the payments would be approximately $6,495.00 per month. That is a large payment to pick up if the tenant defaults on the lease.

There are of course single tenant retail properties priced much lower than this that can provide similar investment benefits. One such benefit is that they are usually located on high-traffic arterial streets. This exposure to traffic and customers is what attracts tenants as they are looking for locations that will make their business successful. It is not the end all but this exposure also makes retail buildings easier to market than those that are located off the beaten path.

Office properties have been my specialty for many years. I heard a speaker at a national conference once state, "The return an investor obtains on an office building is in direct proportion to how he manages the cost of tenant improvements over the life of his investment." This is a true statement. Office buildings do require a high capital investment over their life. Small generic office space layouts will accommodate most tenants without the need for modification. When you start to get over 2,000 square feet, each business will have unique and different space requirements. So, with each new tenant you may be required to gut the space and install new improvements based on their needs. The cost of these improvements varies to some degree whether in small, or large, communities.

Currently in Spokane, it will cost around $10 to $15 per square foot of space to repaint, replace carpet and do other minor improvements for a new or renewing office tenant. Additionally, if you have a tenant who needs a new space configuration, those improvements can cost from $25 to $30 per square foot. A law firm's tenant improvements might cost $50 to $70 per square foot. Medical and dental tenants, with their requirements for extensive plumbing, electrical and cabinetry can cost up to $100 per square foot. Keep in mind economies of scale. Generally speaking, the smaller the space, the higher the cost per square foot and the larger the space, the lower the cost per square foot. We will go into more detail on tenant improvements in Chapter 31.

Office tenants can be long term, stable tenants. Your local dentist, attorney or insurance representative with a mature business might stay in an office building for the majority of their career if they are well taken care of by their landlord. I assisted a dentist in buying an office building after he had leased space in the same building for 27 years. He leased space from another dentist who owned the building and he had never thought about owning his own building.

One other key to obtaining a good return with office

buildings is the ability to manage the day to day operating costs of the building. Many multi-tenant office buildings are leased on a full service basis with most or all of the operating expenses included in the rent. Office tenants prefer knowing exactly what they have to pay each month for the term of their lease. So, you must be a very astute manager to obtain a solid return on your office building investments.

One property type that usually does not have the need for a lot of tenant improvements is industrial. I have developed a number of small industrial buildings over the years. Some of these buildings were divided into small tenant spaces of 1,500 square feet each. They had an overhead door and a man door that led to a small office and bathroom. When a tenant vacated their space we power washed the warehouse floor, cleaned the carpet, painted the office, and we were ready for the next tenant. One disadvantage to buildings like this is that you may have higher tenant turnover. Small industrial tenants tend to outgrow these small bays and you spend more time re-leasing your vacancies. I do like this type of property though, as the smaller bays tend to have high demand and are usually easy to lease. Additionally, if you have a building with five or six bays you usually have a maximum of only one or two vacancies at any one time. If you own a quality building in a well established, high density area it can stay full for a long time with very little vacancy between tenants.

Aside from single family rental homes, residential multi-unit apartment properties are probably where most investors begin their real estate investing. You can start with duplexes or fourplexes and work your way up to larger properties. Many apartment properties can be financed with smaller down payments than commercial properties. Due to their relatively stable income, financial institutions will usually finance apartment properties with around a 20% down payment. Apartments can also be more easily purchased with seller financing.

The beauty of apartments is that the leases are usually short term: as short as month to month, to as long as one year. Short leases allow owners to easily adjust rents up or down to keep units full. Again, with a 24-unit property, you are less likely to have 100% vacancy. A good manager of apartment properties will work hard to quickly adjust rents and keep their units full in the event of economic downturns that affect occupancy. In this recession with many people losing their homes, the apartment market has been very strong due to the demand for rentals from previous home owners.

The flip side of investing in apartment buildings is that they are very management-intensive. It takes more time to rent units, collect rent, deal with problem tenants, and handle the more frequent maintenance issues associated with apartment buildings. When you are starting out you will probably want to handle these responsibilities on your own.

It does take a certain assertive personality type to effectively manage apartment properties. Some of my first investments were small, old apartment buildings. It did not take me long as a young man to determine that dealing with apartment tenants day to day was both very time consuming and was not a personality fit for me. As I mentioned before, I was way too nice to some of my problem tenants, and a number of them took advantage of me. I have learned over time to be much more assertive, but also realized that it was advantageous to hire professional management for my properties. As you progress in your investing, you will be wise to hire professional management, and you'll be glad you did.

Finally, let's talk briefly about land investments. One of the key advantages of investing in land is that it does not take as much management time as properties with tenants. It does, however, take financial capacity if you are making payments when you buy the land. You must be in a position to easily make those payments for a long time if necessary. If you expect to get a good return by investing in land, you must develop it very quickly after you purchase it, or you must buy it real cheap. Since land is not very liquid, it can often be purchased at a very good price. But then, you may have to hold the property for many years to get your money back from it. My partners and I have a number of pieces of land that we have owned for over thirty years. Hopefully, some day we will sell those properties and end up with a profit.

Two key questions may be, "Which property type best fits my risk tolerance and investment objectives?" and "What can I afford to purchase to get started?" As we have discussed, for many investors, the answer might be starting with single-family homes.

On the other hand, many investors I know started in the business by purchasing older, run-down commercial and industrial properties in less expensive areas. These properties may take more work to get fixed up and in good rentable condition. They also might not attract the highest credit tenants but they are a good option for getting a start in the business.

Regardless of the type of property you choose or how you get into it, explore the types of real estate that interest you and learn the tricks of the trade. If you apply yourself and learn all you can about the type of real estate you choose, there is plenty of money to be made.

Buying real estate is not only the best way,
the quickest way, the safest way, but the
only way to become wealthy.
　　　　　　　　　　Marshall Field

~ Notes ~

~ 20 ~
The Reality of Nothing Down

Why would a real estate book written in 2013 have a chapter about buying properties with nothing down? It is hard enough to get a loan for any real estate investment today, let alone try and get highly leveraged financing.

The overall mentality of our nation has changed with the recent recession. Many people, including myself, do not want to get caught in a situation like this again and will be more conservative with our borrowing in the future. Personally, I will be inclined to put *more* money down when I purchase properties.

Even though we are currently in a tight lending market that for most of us is unprecedented, things will ease up over time. And when it comes to real estate, most of us have short memories. It won't be too long before many investors are back trying to obtain as much leverage as they can. There may even be circumstances where I will use leverage if I can safely manage the debt that will be incurred.

But let's explore the "nothing down" program. Many books have been written that advocate buying property with little or no money down. Usually, the idea is this: Accumulate all this property with little or no cash, and when it appreciates in value, you sell it and make a substantial profit.

On the surface, it sounds too good to be true. Well,

guess what? It usually is! This technique might work in a rising market during times of great inflation, but we haven't been in such an economy for some time. Nothing-down deals give an investor a larger monthly payment—and big headaches—if everything doesn't go exactly as planned.

For example, let's say you are able to buy a $1 million building with $100,000 down, which would be considered a highly leveraged transaction. A 20-year loan at a 7% interest rate would give you a monthly payment of about $7,000. Depending on the type of property and other factors, it might be hard to generate enough income from a $1 million property to cover such a steep monthly payment.

For the sake of argument, though, let's say it does cover your monthly payment and expenses. If it's an apartment building, what happens when a major employer in your community lays off a large number of workers and you lose 25% of your tenants? You now have the dubious privilege of coming up with about $2,000 per month to feed your investment until you can fill the units back up. What if it's a single-tenant commercial building and your one-and-only tenant declares bankruptcy? You now have to come up with $7,000 every month to stay current on your payments. That's not quite the sweet deal you thought it would be.

A number of years ago, an investor in my community bought a large, vacant warehouse building for $1.25 million, which was a great price for the property at that time. A local bank lent the investor all the money on a short-term note. He then ordered an appraisal, which came in at $2.7 million, far more than it was really worth.

This was back in the days before the banks ordered the appraisals themselves; now, appraisers are hired by banks in an effort to eliminate any influence from the purchaser.

With that appraisal in hand, the investor went to another bank and secured a $2 million loan on the property. The math is simple: He paid off the short-term note for $1.25 million and now had the building and $750,000 in his pocket tax-free.

That was the good news; here's the bad news. His building was empty, and a with a $2 million loan, he probably had a payment of $15,000 to $16,000 per month. If he could have rented out the building, it would have been the type of no-down investment that many books trumpet. Unfortunately, that wasn't the case. He didn't get the building rented. He couldn't make the payment, and he ended up filing for bankruptcy.

I have a nothing-down story of my own. Years ago, I was marketing a building for sale, for a client who had found a larger building he wanted to buy. We couldn't find a buyer for the old building though, and he couldn't finance the new building without selling the old one. Finally, he said he just wanted someone to take over his mortgage payments for him so he could make his move to the bigger building.

I immediately thought of taking on the payments myself, but at the time, I couldn't afford an extra monthly commitment of $1,250. I found two partners, and together we assumed my client's loans.

With no money down and a measly $313 in closing costs, we thought we had made an incredible deal. After six months of trying unsuccessfully to find a tenant, the "incredible" deal didn't feel so incredible anymore, and the monthly payments of $1,250—just over $400 apiece—started to get old. About then, one partner announced he was out of money and couldn't make his share of the monthly payment anymore. He deeded his interest in the property to the other partner and me, which increased our ownership in the property but also boosted our monthly tab.

The story gets even better—or worse, if you're me. Eighteen months after the initial purchase, we were grateful to have a tenant inked to pay $750 a month. By doing so, we locked in our monthly loss at $500. Eventually, after lengthy negotiations, we refinanced the two loans against the property and increased the tenant's rent to get us close to breaking even each month.

Time does seem to heal a lot of wounds when it comes to real estate. When we finally sold the building to the next-door neighbor a few years later, we actually made some money—not a lot, but at least we didn't take a loss.

The reality of no-money down deals is that, in many instances, harsh consequences may follow. Of course, there are exceptions. Once you become a seasoned investor, you may find a property with all the right ingredients for a nothing-down deal.

Let's say you purchase an empty building for far less than it is worth. Today that might be 60 cents on the dollar. Empty buildings in the current recession are selling at some drastic discounts. Bank repossessions would be a good example. Sometimes a bank is determined to dispose of a property no matter how low the price needs to be to get the property sold. Then you get lucky and find a long-term tenant that is a perfect fit for the property and is willing to pay market rent for the space. The property is now potentially worth its former undiscounted value.

So, if the property appraises at its former value and the bank makes a loan at 60% of the property's value, you have 100% financing. This would only take place if you have excellent credit, a solid real estate borrowing history, and a long term relationship with a bank. This can and does happen!

Exercise great caution when considering nothing-down, get-rich-quick deals. They can create extreme financial hardship in many cases. Remember that lower leverage means lower risk and higher leverage means higher risk. Work to come up with a prudent amount of equity for the solid deals you find. But, also be on the lookout for those once-in-a-lifetime opportunities where nothing down might actually be a safe bet.

Failure is success if we learn from it.
Malcom Forbes

~ Notes ~

~ 21 ~
Partnerships: How to Get Started with Less Cash

There is an alternative to purchasing properties with nothing down that has worked very well for me over the years, and it has a number of benefits. Let's say you scrape together $10,000 to purchase your first investment property. It will be difficult to get into a commercial property for that amount of cash unless you want to be highly leveraged. A commercial real estate investment property in Spokane could be found for $200,000, but now we are back to the almost-nothing-down option, which is high risk.

You can't do much on your own in the commercial investing world with only $10,000. But if you find four other people with $10,000 each, you have $50,000 to put down on a property, and now you have some options. Forming such partnerships is the way many of my mentors built their portfolios and net worth. Some of them bought real estate with a single partner and others put together groups of investors. My mentors would typically take a share of ownership in exchange for finding the property and putting the partnership together. Some of them put in cash just like the other partners and then charged a fee for putting the partnership together.

I have followed this path and it has worked very well for me. It is about pooling your resources with like minded partners to accomplish something as a group that would be difficult to do on your own. Having partners is not without its own set of additional challenges, but it does make it easier to get started in real estate investing. Most of the time, it is much less risky than going with the nothing-down option.

Partnerships have a couple of other benefits as well. First, they allow you to diversify your investing. The old cliché that says "Don't put all your eggs in one basket" applies directly to real estate investing. I would much rather have 20% interests in five buildings than 100% interest in one building. It spreads out the risk. Additionally, as partners you are usually able to combine your resources and purchase better properties. The larger properties are also more cost effective to have professionally managed. You get some natural economies of scale. It is a great way to begin building a diversified investment portfolio starting with small amounts of cash.

I have one investor friend who has been putting together partnerships for the last two years to purchase foreclosed, single- family homes. He and his partners pay cash for homes in the $40,000 to $70,000 range. With each purchase, each partner invests $5,000 to $10,000. By paying cash, they have no concerns about making monthly mortgage payments, and they can be very selective with the tenants they pick for the homes. When repairs are needed, they chip in the cash for those as well. Once they get a home rented to a good tenant, they begin looking for another one to buy.

When I started investing over thirty years ago, my partners and I began by chipping in $500 to $1,000 each for down payments on inexpensive pieces of industrial land located in what we believed was the path of progress.

We speculated that those properties would have robust appreciation. Once we closed on a property, we'd each chip in $25 to $50 for the monthly payments and expenses. Through the years, we worked our way up to larger properties, each contributing $5,000, then $10,000, then $25,000, and eventually $50,000 or more.

The days of chipping in $500 each are in the past; a lot of things have changed since then. In Spokane, though, there have always been plenty of great commercial real estate investment options in the $150,000 to $1 million price range—and that's still true today! In fact, sometimes there are great deals in that price range because many investors overlook the lower end of the market.

If you live in a large metropolitan area, commercial property prices might be beyond your reach, but you can still invest in mid-sized cities. Many investors from Seattle and California have had great success investing in Spokane throughout the years.

One quick note of clarification: I call them partnerships, but that typically isn't the legal structure of the real estate investment groups I establish. Today, most investment groups form a limited-liability company (LLC) as the ownership entity for each real estate purchase. An LLC protects the partners and limits the liability of the partners in any adverse actions that might happen to that entity. As an example, if you own an apartment building in an LLC and someone slips on an icy sidewalk, falls and sues the owners, that suit is limited to the LLC ownership entity. There is protection from the tenant suing you personally.

In this area, it is especially important to get good legal

advice before you begin forming any partnerships. The laws regarding the structure of partnerships vary from state to state, so make sure your legal counsel is well acquainted with the laws in your state.

Through the years, I've been involved in around 50 partnerships and have gleaned some insights that are helpful when forming such alliances. Here are some important things I've learned along the way:

- **Six or fewer partners are preferred.** While I've been involved with partnerships of up to 12 partners at a time, I've found that having fewer partners makes it less complicated. It is easier for a smaller number of investors to maintain the same investment goals and to resolve different issues as they arise.
- **Partnerships aren't for everyone.** They take a large investment of time, effort and communication. Pick partners who are team players and who have realistic expectations.
- **Underpromise and overdeliver.** I will go the extra mile to make sure my partners are treated fairly at all times, and to structure partnerships that treat them the way I would want to be treated. You must view your partners like customers, because that's just what they are. If you get greedy, it will undermine the investment and the partnership.
- **Honesty is key.** For me, everything is an open book, and I do my best to keep my partners informed at all times. If you have consistent,

honest communication, it is much easier to maintain your partners' support when it is needed.

- **Real estate is a problem-prone business.** Always educate prospective partners on the potential pitfalls of the business, and that issues will come up over the life of the investment. When—not if—problems arise, inform your partners quickly. If you need cash, give them plenty of warning as soon as you can. No one likes surprises.

- **Clearly define goals and expectations to your partners.** Make sure that all the partners realize that real estate investing is a long term proposition. I am not a speculator trying to get in and out quickly. I started out telling my partners that they should plan on having their money tied up for at least five years. Later, I shifted to telling them that we would hold the property until the mortgage was paid off, and then we would continue to hold the property for retirement income.

Over the last thirty years, I have experienced some of the normal problems that arise with partnerships. I have had four partners go through a divorce. Two of them needed to be bought out; we arrived at a fair price for their shares, and the other partners bought them out. In the third divorce situation, my partner settled with his wife and he is still my partner today. In the fourth case, my partner settled with his wife, and she retained the partnership interest.

I have had some partners end up in financial trouble

unrelated to our real estate investments. One of those partners deeded his interest in the partnership to the remaining partners. In the other case, we arrived at a fair price for the partner's share and bought him out. Partnership agreements have provisions for dealing with such problems and buying out partners if it becomes necessary.

With a couple of my partnerships we put a value on the partnership at each annual meeting. This practice keeps the valuation current which would, in the event of a divorce or death, make it easier to settle ownership among us. Thankfully to date, I have not had a partner pass away, but I do make sure there are provisions in my partnership agreements in case an unfortunate situation like that takes place.

I have been very fortunate to have collaborated with some wonderful partners in the last thirty years. In fact, the majority of them have become some of my best friends. As the normal problems of real estate ownership have come our way we have worked through them in a professional manner and maintained our friendships. I am very thankful to have enjoyed such great relationships with my investment partners. They are outstanding, loyal people who have stuck with me through good times and bad.

If you treat your partners well as I believe I have done, they will come back again and again as more opportunities come along and you grow your investments over time. Together, you can be on the lookout for lucrative investments. The good deals are out there, and I will share some of my super deals with you a little later in this book. The more properties you own, the greater the odds are that you'll latch onto that stellar performer: one that will make more money for you and your partners than any no-down deal ever could—more than you ever dreamed.

The best investment on earth is earth.
Louis Glickman

~ Notes ~

~ 22 ~
Financing: A Whole New Ball Game

When it comes to financing investment real estate, we are in unprecedented times. The lending pendulum has swung further to the conservative side than I have ever seen it before—and it seems to be stuck there. This situation is causing major distress for many real estate investors who find themselves over-leveraged and in a financial pinch.

While challenges have been created by recessions for some investors, they also generate amazing opportunities for others. There is going to be another great exchange of wealth in the U.S. during the next few years, from real estate investors who are forced to sell, to those with cash who are ready to buy. We are already seeing it in many parts of the market. Investors who have cash and the ability to obtain financing are making some unbelievable buys in today's market from investors who are over-leveraged and forced to sell. But where and how does an investor obtain financing in this unusual economy?

It's a totally new ballgame securing real estate financing after the recession of 2008, 2009 and 2010. The rules have changed substantially from any previous recession I have experienced in my career. As with any other economic cycle, lending and other market conditions will stabilize. The pendulum will swing back to a place of normalcy, except normal might not include the super-easy money we saw in prior boom times.

Today, unless you have a long-standing relationship with financial institutions that make commercial real estate loans, it is difficult to secure financing for investment real estate. Lenders are saying they will not finance some types of properties at all—properties such as hotels that, from the bank's perspective, have a high degree of risk attached to them in a down economy.

Even if you are fortunate enough to have good credit and a strong relationship with a banker, you still might have to put up 30% to 40% of the purchase price of the property as the down payment to obtain a loan. Previously, the banks would have considered making a loan on investment real estate with a 15% to 20% down payment. These stiff lending requirements have taken a lot of real estate investors out of the market.

Secondary lenders such as life insurance companies provided financing for real estate investment properties in recent years, but usually in loan amounts over a million dollars. During the downturn, many of these secondary lenders have been sitting on the sidelines waiting for things to shake out. They will eventually be back in the market; it's just a matter of when. So there is much less investment real estate lending happening, and the lending that is being done is on very stiff terms.

Let's talk about some things to keep in mind in a typical lending market. I do believe that when things return to some semblance of normal, those investors with good credit, a solid borrowing track record and an attractive financial statement will find it easier to secure loans. The new norm might be 25% down instead of the 15% down that was possible in the past, and that's probably a good thing. Many of us will take a more conservative approach to our borrowing, and I believe most of us will want to borrow less after surviving this economic cycle. Personally, I plan to take a more conservative approach to my real estate investing and am thinking about putting together some debt-free real estate investment partnerships. I do know that I am going to be more averse to taking on debt than I was in the past, no matter how risk-free a deal looks.

In a more stable lending market, there are three primary ways to finance investment real estate: conventional commercial loans, secondary-market loans and seller financing.

Conventional Commercial Loans

As we've discussed, most banks or credit unions will now require a down payment of 30% to 40%. If you are fortunate enough to have a lot of liquid assets and a solid borrowing history, lenders may relax their down payment requirements slightly. Some bankers might provide a second mortgage on another asset or provide a line of credit that you can borrow against to come up with part of the down payment. The time frame for a line of credit loan will likely be as short as one or two years at the most. So for most of us, it will require a more significant amount of cash to be an active real estate investor.

I believe that your equity in a property should correspond with the property's level of risk. High risk properties should be purchased with a high amount of equity. Likewise, low-risk properties would allow for a lower amount of equity. For example, if you have a creditworthy tenant with a long-term lease, a smaller down payment might be fine. Your risk of vacancy is small and it is unlikely that you will find yourself saddled with making the monthly payments on your own. If a building has high vacancy or high-risk tenants, I would recommend putting more money down and have lower monthly payments. This will minimize the amount of money you have to come up with out of pocket if and when the building does have vacancies.

Because my investment philosophy has always been to pay off mortgages quickly, my goal is to get as short an amortization period—the gradual elimination of real estate debt—as possible. I suggest structuring the amortization to yield a reasonable amount of cash flow, some of which should go into a savings account to address a worst-case scenario should it occur.

In the past, if I was able to purchase a property at a good value, and if interest rates were low enough and rents were high enough, I sought to obtain a loan that amortized in 15 years. If all the variables lined up, this was entirely possible, and I am sure it will be possible again in the future. Having mortgages that amortize in 15 years really helps you reach the goal of having paid-for buildings.

In 1997 an investor told me that he and his partners were thinking of selling a small office building they had owned for about ten years. At the time, the price they wanted was at the top of, or even above, the market. The building was in good condition, was occupied by a creditworthy tenant, and was in an excellent location. Interest rates were around 8.5 to 9%. I liked the property but not the price the investors were asking. I stayed in contact with them for about a year. They never formally offered the property for sale, but kept mentioning to a number of other potential buyers that they were interested in selling.

As the year passed, interest rates all of a sudden began to move downward. I called a local lender I knew and asked what terms he would offer me on a loan for this property. He said that rates had dropped to under 8% and that they would continue to slide in the next sixty days. I quickly made an offer to the owners to buy the building at the price they had been asking, subject to obtaining a loan. I ended up with a loan at an interest rate of 6.91%! This swing in interest rates had turned an overpriced property into one with great cash flow. With the lower interest rates the loan payments were lower. This enabled my partners and me to obtain a loan with a 20-year amortization and still have excellent cash flow. So, financing in this case was the key to buying a quality property.

Let's talk about the ins and outs of obtaining a commercial real estate loan in more detail. The main elements you need to consider are: the down payment and the length of the loan amortization, which we have talked about; the interest rate; the loan term; and the loan fees and costs.

Interest rates set by banks and other conventional commercial lenders are typically fixed for specific time frames such as five, seven, or ten years. They do not want to lock into interest rates for long periods of time when rates may increase and leave them with below-market returns. Therefore, lenders will usually charge lower rates for a shorter interest rate lock, which allows them to adjust the interest rates as the market changes. For instance, rates locked in for five years will be lower than those locked in for seven or ten years. When you obtain financing, you need to choose a time frame to lock in your interest rate based on the level of risk you are willing to take that interest rates will go up or down.

In the past, I took a conservative approach and locked in most of my commercial mortgages for longer time frames like ten years. There can be a cost to taking the conservative approach, though. Today I have some old mortgages that I locked in long term at 8.5%, wanting to cover myself if rates went higher. When lenders lock in a rate for you, they will usually not allow you to prepay the mortgage if rates go down without charging you a penalty. The lender has spent time and money to place their money in the market, and they want to get the interest yield that they have locked in. So as a borrower, you need to wait until the end of the loan, or pay the penalty to pay off the loan early.

Many loans I have gotten in the last several years have been for a term of less than ten years. The amortization is usually longer than ten years, but the term of the loan is three, five or seven years. With shorter term loans you usually get a much lower interest rate, but you take on the risk that rates could be adjusted upward at the end of the loan term. So, if you think rates are going to go down, take a short term loan. If you think rates are going up, you want to lock in for the long haul.

When you buy a property, consider how the ups and downs of interest rates during the time you own the property will affect your investment. When interest rates are low, you should lock them in as long as you can. When they are high, you may want a shorter term loan that gives you the flexibility of refinancing the property at a lower rate of interest in the future.

Upfront fees for these types of loans, which a lender charges for making the loan, usually run from 1/2 to 2% of the amount borrowed, or $5,000 to $20,000 for a $1 million loan. In addition to the loan fee, there are closing costs such as document preparation fees or legal fees, title insurance and other related fees. In a normal market, I usually go to a number of lenders and get up to three quotes for a particular loan. It's to your advantage to create some competition for your business among lenders, with the goal of getting the best loan and terms possible. Unfortunately, in today's market, it might be tough to find lenders who will compete for your business unless you are a seasoned real estate investor.

Having solid professional relationships with multiple lenders is important and will give you more options over time. Lending policies at different institutions can and will change. A lender might go after commercial loans aggressively for a period of time, then pull back and tighten its lending criteria. If this is the case, it's good to be well acquainted with other lenders who might be more eager to get money out the door.

Secondary-Market Loans

The next type of financing comes from the secondary market, which consists of life insurance companies and other large national lenders. Due to their size, they typically won't consider loans less than $1 million. While these loan processes are similar to conventional loans, the borrower that meets their minimum requirements is required to fill out more paperwork to complete a loan than at a conventional bank or credit union. The upfront cost of obtaining financing is usually higher as well.

The main benefit of using secondary lenders is that they can usually provide lower rates of interest that can be fixed for longer periods of time. For example, you might be able to obtain a loan with an interest rate that is fixed for 15 or 20 years. If you have a property that requires a $1 million-plus loan and you plan to hold the property for a long time, the secondary market is where you want to look. The savings created by a slightly lower interest rate can add up to a lot of money over time.

An additional benefit of using a secondary market lender is the possibility of obtaining **non-recourse financing**. Non-recourse financing is when the lender agrees to only take back the property as their recourse in the case of default. Secondary lenders will provide non-recourse financing if your down payment is large enough and the property meets certain lending criteria.

With most lenders you will need to personally guarantee a commercial real estate loan. So, if things go bad and you give the property back to the bank, they have the ability to sell the property and go after you personally for any loss they incur. This loss is called a **deficiency judgment**. Not a fun situation in a worst case scenario, so non-recourse financing can be an important consideration in some cases.

Many large developers try to obtain non-recourse financing for projects that have a high degree of risk. Then, if the project fails they are not at risk of losing all of their personal assets. They only lose the cash they have put into the project. In some instances, you can find secondary lenders that will make loans for less than $1 million, so it's worth considering the secondary market for a loan as you are weighing your options.

Seller Financing

In this case, the seller is asked to finance the property. In the markets where I work, this practice is less prevalent than it was 20 to 25 years ago. That said, seller financing is more common on land purchases where conventional financing is harder to obtain.

With seller financing, the loan is not restricted to industry norms, and the terms can be whatever you negotiate. I have been involved in some very creative seller financing through the years. Once, I arranged a seller-financed transaction with a 40-year amortization and no balloon payment. I have done some deals where the owner agreed to take the first half of the down payment at closing and the balance a year later. There can be dramatically more flexible options created in these arrangements. As long as all of the parties in the transaction can come to terms, nearly any sort of arrangement is possible.

With the current tight lending standards imposed by banks, we are seeing many more seller-financed investment property sales. A benefit to the sellers is that they can receive a very attractive interest rate on the equity they have built up in their property. I am currently seeing seller financing agreed to at interest rates in the range of 5–8%. This is a much greater return than many sellers will find on a conservative bond or security investment. And, the seller has the property as security for the loan.

While there are three primary avenues for financing

investments, there is also a fourth, rather unenviable option. Many people who don't have good credit and who put together high-risk real estate investments tend to end up in a fourth lending arena called **hard-money loans**. These borrowers end up paying higher interest rates and fees to get real estate loans from small loan companies and private individuals. I recall an investor a few years ago who had purchased a piece of land for $300,000 cash. His cash flow situation had taken a wrong turn and he desperately needed to access some of the cash he had used to buy the land. During the recession, none of the banks wanted to lend money on anything that did not have solid cash flow, namely land. After being turned down by numerous banks, the investor began looking into his hard money borrowing options. The best offer he got was a $100,000 loan at 14% interest with loan fees and costs totaling about $15,000. That is expensive money!

You might assume that hard money borrowers are typically just getting started in the business and do small projects. In fact, they are often investors who have been in the business for many years; some of them have millions of dollars of net worth. They may have very little liquidity, blemished credit, or a history of doing high-risk projects, some of which have failed.

My recommendation: Don't go down this path. There are very few real estate investments that are so good that they justify obtaining a hard money loan. Work hard to maintain solid credit and only go after projects that have a reasonable chance of success with conventional financing.

Regardless of the financing method, the more times

you borrow money, the more you learn about the process and the more comfortable you get signing your name to the lengthy documents that are required.

Your goal should be to get the best interest rate and lowest fee package possible for each loan. Each loan should be structured to suit the specific property you are acquiring and the level of risk attached to that property. Over time, the cost of borrowing will be a key factor in determining the return your real estate investment yields. So, learn to be a prudent and knowledgeable borrower.

Mortgage and borrow when things are looking good.
Craig McCaw

~ Notes ~

~ 23 ~
Real Estate Math 101

I won't go so far as to say everything you need to know about real estate investing you learned in grade school. But you did learn one of the most crucial skills: basic math.

Analyzing a real estate investment is nothing more than one big math problem. You gather all of the facts and figures. You complete the calculations, and you weigh them with reality to come to a conclusion.

Fortunately for those in the real estate industry, it's not calculus. It's a simple math problem that calls for addition, subtraction, multiplication and division. While simple, it's absolutely critical that you get it right.

The most common math problem an investor faces is determining what a property is worth. To be a skilled investor, you must gain enough market knowledge to do the math quickly to determine a property's current value and its future earning potential. Quickly assessing a property's value allows you to act, taking advantage of an opportunity that might disappear if you don't move expediently. Sense of urgency aside, your time is valuable, and you shouldn't spend a lot of time on due diligence if the numbers don't work.

One tool that many investors use to assist them in doing real estate investment math is a basic financial calculator. Many real estate investors I know are still using the trusty old Hewlett Packard 12C which first came out in 1981. The 12C was the world's first horizontal financial calculator. This amazing little machine has been an industry mainstay. The 12C uses what is called reverse Polish notation which can take a little getting used to. Like most financial calculators the 12C contains mortgage amortization tables which are key tools for real estate investment analysis. You can still purchase a 12C for around $60. Just think of it as a very worthwhile investment.

So let's begin. Our first goal is to establish the actual income potential of a property. If leases with tenants have been in place for a long time with minimal or no rent increases, the rental rates might be below market value. Conversely, leases that have rent-increase clauses ultimately could take a tenant's rent well above market rates. While that is good for a landlord, it's unlikely a new owner of the property could command a similar lease rate from a new tenant in the future. Sometimes, a building owner offers a tenant free rent as an incentive to lease space and pay the owners asking rental rate. That free rent may allow the building owner to achieve an above market rent.

Here's an example: During a stagnant market in the 1980s, a Seattle developer renovated an office building in downtown Spokane. He asked for lease rates of $16 per square foot annually, even though there were plenty of comparable spaces available in other buildings that were being marketed for $2 to $4 less per square foot. When he had no takers, he changed his approach. He offered free rent for one year and annual lease rates of $17 per square foot for the following two years if a tenant signed a three-year lease. It worked. With the free rent up front, he started to attract tenants into the building.

The developer's goal in giving the free rent up front was to achieve the highest rent possible in the second two years of the lease. There are a couple of major benefits to this approach. First, a year down the road, a building owner could attempt to value his property based on the $17-per-square-foot rents. Also, when it comes time to renew leases, those tenants are accustomed to paying the above-market rents. They are settled in, and moving would be costly. Unless there is an abundance of vacant space at lower rents nearby, it will be easier for them to renew their leases—even at the above-market rent—rather than move. This is a common practice by developers to achieve the highest value possible for their projects.

A knowledgeable buyer or appraiser would know to navigate past such a situation, but some less experienced buyers may not. To determine the actual value of a building, you have to know what real market rents are for a property. Factors in determining market rents include building amenities, parking, views, location, exposure, traffic counts and who—landlord or tenant—pays what expenses. Market conditions weigh in as well. The more time and experience you amass in real estate, the more quickly and confidently you'll be able to figure out what rent should be charged. If you are new to real estate investing, a knowledgeable commercial real estate broker can assist you in this process.

With a market rent in hand, you can apply that rent to the size of the building and determine how much income the property can ultimately produce.

There's another question to ask at this stage: Are you

charging rent for useable area or rentable area? Useable area is the area actually occupied by tenants. Rentable area consists of useable area *plus* each tenant's share of the common area.

The amount of common area attributed to each tenant varies depending upon the design of the building. However, as a general rule, the common area charged to a tenant doesn't exceed 15% of the square footage of useable space. This common area percentage is referred to as a **load factor**. You can say a tenant's share of the common area is loaded onto the useable space.

For example, if a company occupies 1,000 square feet of useable space and has a 15% load factor, it would be accountable for 150 square feet of common space—and charged rent on a total of 1,150 square feet of space. The tenant would pay rent on 15% more space than they occupy, or 115% of their useable square footage.

Useable square footage: 1,000
Load factor multiplier: x 115%
Rentable Square footage: 1,150

The Building Owners and Managers Association International (BOMA) has worked with architects to refine the standards for measuring buildings using useable and rentable guidelines. Again, understanding the math and related measurements is important in assessing the income generating capacity of a building.

Once the projected income is in hand, vacancies need to be figured into the equation. Even if a building is fully leased at present, it's unlikely that it will remain fully occupied during the time you own it. Real estate appraisers use a vacancy factor in evaluating a property. Such vacancy rates can vary from 5 to 10%, and can be even higher in some instances. We could spend a whole chapter on the nuances of determining a vacancy factor, but again, seasoned brokers can help.

After that, we move to operating expenses. WARNING: This is the area where most investors get themselves into trouble. They don't do enough homework to determine the actual expenses involved in owning and operating a property. First, look at all the apparent expenses for which records are easy to find: taxes, insurance, utilities, janitorial and day-to-day maintenance. Next, ask the seller for their last three years of operating expense records. If you suspect those aren't accurate—or you just want to make sure—request to see the schedule from their income tax return that relates to the property.

Of course, real estate professionals can give you local rule-of-thumb numbers. For example, when all of the expenses are factored in, it typically costs between $5 and $7 per square foot annually to operate a single- or two-story suburban office building in Spokane, Washington.

One last component which I discussed in Chapter 7— reserves for replacements—is often underestimated or left out entirely by eager investors. This is a mistake. As a building owner, you must factor in funds for updates and repairs. Over the life of your real estate investment you will have capital expenses such as roofs, heating, ventilation and air conditioning units and parking lot recoating and striping. Maintaining your property in good condition will help preserve your investment.

Keep this in mind: Many buyers might ignore some costs or reserves and pay more for a building than good math suggests would be prudent. Don't fall into this trap. Always remember, you make money when you buy, so you want to be conservative and as accurate as possible with your calculations.

After gathering as much information as you can on a property's income, vacancy, and expenses you can do a quick analysis of its value like the example below. Take your best estimate of the property's income, adjust for a market vacancy rate and subtract your best estimate of the property's expenses. Then take the resulting net operating income (NOI) and apply an appropriate cap rate. This should give you a quick but accurate estimate of the property's market value.

Projected Annual Income:	$163,468
Vacancy and Credit Loss:	($8,173)
Effective Gross Income:	$155,296
Annual Operating Expenses:	($48,356)
Net Operating Income:	$106,940
Cap Rate:	7.5%
Indicated Value/Estimated Value:	$1,425,000

With an estimate of the property's market value in hand you can now determine how much you are willing to pay for the property. The goal is to do a **quick** analysis of the property and get an offer to the seller. As we have discussed, timing can be a big advantage in real estate investing. If the math makes sense, you want to get your offer in as soon as possible without appearing to be anxious. If you are able to come to an agreement with the seller, then you can do your due diligence and work to confirm and fine tune your math.

The Income Approach to Value chart on the next page provides a more complete picture of a property's projected value. Based on a real property my partners and I evaluated, it shows the detail necessary when fully analyzing a property after you are under a contract to purchase. You can also go into this much detail before you make an offer **if** you have time and the seller has provided the information needed. The more sophisticated the property, the more study is necessary before making an offer. Like they say, "The devil is in the details." You will need to be both Sherlock Holmes to dig up all of the facts, and then be proficient in basic math to complete your study of the property.

As the Income Approach to Value shows, the project penciled out, and my partners and I made the purchase. According to my math, this will be a solid long-term investment for us.

This book covers most of the concepts detailed in the Income Approach to Value example in this chapter. In order to become a successful real estate investor you will need to understand and run these kinds of projections with ease on a regular basis. So take time to study and become a real estate investment math whiz. It will pay big returns in the long run!

INCOME APPROACH TO VALUE

216 North Atlas Road
Spokane, WA

REVENUES

Base Rental Income	Total NRA	Contract Rent Per SF/YR	Market Rent Per SF/YR	Annual Rent
XO Testing	2,021	$19.41		$39,228
ADF	1,863	$20.00		$37,260
Vacant	4,349		$20.00	$86,980
	8,233			
		$19.85		$163,468

Potential Gross Income (PGI):				**$163,468**
Less Stabalized Vacancy/Credit Loss:	5.0% x PGI of	$163,468		($8,173)
Effective Gross Income (EGI):		**$19.04/SF**		**$155,296**

EXPENSES	Annual Amount	$/SF of Total NRA	
Real Estate Taxes	$16,000	$1.94	
Insurance	$2,882	$0.35	
Utilities (W/S/E/G)	$10,291	$1.25	
Janitorial	$8,233	$1.00	
Parking Lot/Landscaping	$2,058	$0.25	
Repair & Maintenance	$4,117	$0.50	
Management Expenses	$3,952	$0.48	
Reserves	823	$0.10	
Total Expenses	$48,356	$5.87	$48,356

Net Operating Income (NOI): $12.99/SF
$106,940

Valuation of Income

Net Operating Income:	$106,940
Capitalization Rate: 7.50%	
Indicated Value:	$1,425,867
Reconciled Value, rounded:	$1,425,000 $173/SF of NRA

~ 24 ~
Cap Rates and NOIs

We've talked about basic math being one important aspect of successful real estate investing. Well, for many investors one of the key math problems is determining the appropriate capitalization rate, or **cap rate** for short, as they evaluate a property.

If you don't know what cap rates are, you aren't alone. Colleagues have told me about investors with millions of dollars in real estate holdings who repeatedly ask how cap rates work. Those investors might not remember how to calculate a cap rate, but they do know that the cap rate is an essential factor in a successful real estate investment.

Simply put, a cap rate is the rate of return an investor uses to convert the **net operating income** (NOI) of a property into its estimated market value. In other words, the NOI is capitalized at a desired rate of return to determine what the investor would be willing to pay for the property. The cap rate is your cash on cash rate of return on a property that was purchased with all cash and no debt. It is one of the many tools used by investors, bankers, and appraisers to evaluate investment real estate and determine its market value.

Before we dig deep into cap rates, there is another way to assess a property's value, and that is to calculate the price per square foot or price per unit. One very prosperous Spokane apartment investor has succeeded by making her apartment purchases based primarily on the price per unit of the properties she considers. For example, if a 48-unit apartment property is available for $2,400,000 then the asking price works out to $50,000 per unit. The sale price is divided by the number of units in the project. This method has apparently worked very well for her, but the cap rate is still one of the most common and reliable methods for determining the value of an income property. In fact, if you were to browse the commercial property for sale ads in the Wall Street Journal, you would see properties advertised for sale by their cap rates.

To explore cap rates, we must first determine the property's NOI. Again, NOI is the revenue a property produces or is projected to produce after all rents are collected, all expenses are paid, and vacancies are factored in. The 216 North Atlas Road property featured in the IAV chart in the previous chapter has a projected NOI of $106,940, which would be your cash flow if you are fortunate to have no mortgage on the property. Otherwise, the NOI is used to make your mortgage payment, and what is left would be your cash flow.

As an investor, banker or appraiser, you will apply a cap rate to the NOI to determine the value of the property. This cap rate will vary depending on the type of property, its location, the quality of the tenants, the length of the leases, and many other factors. Keep in mind that cap rates are somewhat arbitrary. They are based on each individual investor's assessment of a property and that investor's desired return. You may be willing to value a property based on a 7% cap rate and I may require 8% to even consider the property.

For example, let's say that you are a seasoned investor

and have specialized in purchasing properties leased to Walgreens. You know what kind of return you can get from a Walgreens property and you closely follow the sale of all Walgreens properties. Your return parameters will probably be different from those of a new investor whose past investments have consisted mostly of bank CDs earning 1–2%. So, cap rates for a specific property will vary to some degree from one investor to another.

When you are working with a cap rate, remember that the NOI of a given property is the constant in the equation. The estimated value will go up and down and the cap rate can be adjusted, but the NOI will remain the same. For example, let's say the NOI from a given property is $100,000. I find concepts easier to convey and to grasp when even numbers are used! The chart below shows the inverse relationship between the cap rate and estimated value with the fixed portion being the NOI.

NOI	Cap Rate	Estimated Value
$100,000	6%	$1,666,666
$100,000	7%	$1,428,571
$100,000	8%	$1,125,000
$100,000	9%	$1,111,111
$100,000	10%	$1,000,000

You can see that if you desire a greater return on your money, the amount you are willing to pay for a property goes down. The reverse is also true: The lower the return you are willing to accept, the more you are willing to pay for the property. Hopefully, this chart makes the inverse relationship between cap rates and estimated values easier to understand.

You divide the NOI you estimate the property will produce by the cap rate you think is appropriate for the property, to determine what you will pay for the property. Calculate the risk involved along with the property characteristics as you weight the appropriate cap rate for the property. Investors will consider a lower cap rate, or a lower rate of return, for quality properties with solid, long-term tenants. They will demand a higher cap rate, or higher rate of return, for poorer quality properties in secondary locations with less creditworthy tenants. Consequently, cap rates will vary depending on the unique characteristics of a property and the location and market in which it is located.

Cap rates currently vary from 6–8% for high quality properties and from 10–12% for higher risk properties. Cap rates tend to move up and down over the years in relationship to interest rates. In some ways, cap rates are similar to credit: a borrower with good credit and a strong down payment gets a lower interest rate on a loan than a borrower with poor credit and little money down.

With the 216 North Atlas Road example from Chapter 23, a cap rate of 7.5% was used to determine the estimated value of $1,425,867. The math equation looks like this:

$$\text{NOI } (\$106,940) \div \text{Cap Rate } (7.5\%)$$
$$= \text{Estimated Value } (\$1,425,867)$$

So, an investor is saying that he or she would be willing to pay a price for the property that will produce a return of 7.5%, with the projected NOI. Let's say that the investor has evaluated the property and believes a 9% return is more appropriate due to the property's location, condition and tenants. The equation would be as follows:

$$\text{NOI } (\$106,940) \div \text{Cap Rate } (9\%)$$
$$= \text{Estimated Value } (\$1,188,222)$$

The estimated value changes by $237,645! You can see that as the cap rate required by the investor goes up, the value of the property goes down. Again, the reverse is, true: as the return, or cap rate, the investor will consider goes down, the value of the property goes up.

The interest rate at which one can borrow money is the next factor in the equation. You always want to borrow money at an interest rate that's less than the cap rate. This is called **positive leverage**. If you borrow money at an interest rate that is greater than the cap rate, that is called **negative leverage**. When the market was booming in the mid-2000s, many investors bid up the price of properties so high that many people were buying properties using negative leverage. This is one reason the real estate market got into the troubles it's currently digging out of.

Once again, having good math skills is one key to making solid real estate investments. I have seen a lot of people get into trouble because either they didn't understand the math or wouldn't take the time to learn it. Math has always been easy for me, but even if numbers aren't your strong suit, the math concepts used in real estate investing are relatively easy to learn.

As for cap rates, the more time you spend analyzing properties, the more you will become familiar with how to determine the appropriate cap rate for different properties. You are then in a position to quickly evaluate properties and determine what you are willing to pay for them. Having a clear understanding of cap rates will allow you to quickly make good real estate investment decisions.

The Certified Commercial Investment Member Institute of the National Association of Realtors (CCIM) has a fabulous course (CI101) that covers all the key math equations used in real estate investing. I highly recommend taking this class if you are serious about real estate investing. You can learn more about the institute and its offerings by visiting their website, which I have listed in Appendix C.

Buy in bad times on good economics and
Sell in good times on bad economics.
                              Author unknown

~ 25 ~
Debt Coverage Ratios

Each individual real estate investment is like its own business. One of the key goals in any business is to make a profit, and in real estate investing part of that profit comes in the form of cash flow. The goal is to maximize your income, minimize your expenses and manage your debt. Through that process, you hopefully create optimal cash flow, or what's commonly referred to in business as a high profit margin or a good spread—the difference between the cost of your product and what you sell it for.

When you finance investment real estate, the lender will require you to show a margin between the annual net operating income the property generates and the annual mortgage payments. In the lending world, this margin is called the **debt-coverage ratio**. The lender wants to make sure you are generating more cash flow from the property than is necessary to cover the mortgage payment. This provides the lender with a margin of safety and helps ensure that you will still be able to make your mortgage payment if unforeseen problems arise with the operation of your property. The bank wants to be sure you are not over-leveraged or borrowing beyond the property's capacity to cover the mortgage payments.

The debt-coverage ratio required by a lender used to be in the range of 1.2 to 1.3 for many types of properties. Today, we are seeing lenders requiring debt coverage ratios of 1.4 or 1.5. Lenders have raised that standard, just like they've raised the standard for down payments. In the past, a bank might have required a down payment as small as 20% of the appraised value of the property. In tighter lending markets, down payments required may be around 30% to 40% of the appraised value.

To see how a debt-coverage ratio works, let's use the earlier example of the property at 216 North Atlas Road from Chapters 23 and 24. Let's say that you had agreed to purchase the North Atlas Road property for $1.4 million. With a down payment of 40%, you would need to borrow $840,000, or 60% of the purchase price. If you could borrow that amount at a 7% interest rate and with payments amortized over 25 years, the annual mortgage payments would be just over $5,900 a month, or $70,830 a year. With a required debt-coverage ratio of 1.5, or 150% of the $70,830 annual mortgage payments, the net operating income (NOI) required from the property would need to be at least $106,245. The annual NOI from that property is $106,940, so there is an adequate margin to satisfy the lender.

You can run this equation in reverse as well. If you have the annual NOI from a property, you can divide it by the debt-coverage ratio to determine the maximum annual mortgage payment a lender will allow.

If you take the NOI of $106,940 and divide it by 1.5, you get $71,293. So the maximum annual debt service that the lender will allow is $71,293, which works out to a monthly mortgage payment of $5,941. Once you have determined the monthly mortgage payment, you can work backward with a financial calculator to determine how much you can borrow if you know the current interest rate and amortization time frame. Using a 7% interest rate and 25 years of amortization, you could borrow $845,493, which falls just above the 60%-of-appraised-value criteria. In this example, the outcome is about the same regardless of whether you move forward or backward.

The lender's first requirement will be to make a loan based on a maximum of 60% of the appraised value of the property. Banks typically base their loan on the agreed-to purchase price or the appraised value, whichever is lower. Then they establish the monthly mortgage payments based on their debt-coverage ratio guidelines. Depending on the lender's overall lending criteria, there may be some flexibility in both of these guidelines, but the lending guidelines today are much more stringent than in the past. In some cases, if the income is not high enough to meet the required debt-coverage ratio, the amount the bank will lend you may be reduced.

So understanding how the debt-coverage ratio works is another important part of the real estate math equation. As you are considering a property to purchase and you determine the NOI, you will be able to quickly determine the maximum loan payments that a lender will approve.

*Real estate is always the best investment in the
world, if you give it time to mature. I never met
anyone who didn't make a lot of money by holding
something for five years.*
William Bone

~ 26 ~
The Magic of Leverage

In real estate investing, the term **leverage** is thrown around quite a bit. In simplest terms, leverage is the use of borrowed capital to increase the potential return on the cash you actually invested. By leveraging, you maximize the return on your own capital by borrowing from others to buy real estate. Leverage can be a powerful tool—if managed properly.

Many of the get-rich-quick concepts in other books suggest that a person should use maximum leverage to attain real estate investing success. In a perfect world, the get-rich-quick program would work like this: You borrow $1 million with nothing down to purchase real estate; then you collect rent from the tenants to pay off the $1 million. Or, the value of your real estate holdings goes up and you sell for a profit. Then ta-da, you are rich.

It sounds good, and yes, it has been done before. It can work as long as the economy is in a period of steep inflation, and prices are rising. Take a look at what happened in the years 2008 through 2011: Our country went into a huge recession and real estate prices fell dramatically! Those who were highly leveraged went broke fast. It has been one of the biggest real estate busts in the history of the U.S. Now, the next part of the cycle starts to kick in and those who have capital are making some great buys on properties from desperate sellers. These investors will make a bundle during the next up cycle.

The Leverage Comparison Chart below illustrates how leverage works. It shows the difference between high, moderate, and no leverage. The high-leverage example is where we were in the mid-2000s. Money was plentiful and easy to borrow. Investors regularly borrowed 80–100% of a property's cost when they made purchases.

Leverage Comparison

Showing No-, Average-, and High- Leverage Returns

	None	Average	High
Net Operating Income (NOI)	$90,000	$90,000	$90,000
Cap Rate	9%	9%	9%
Value	$1,000,000	$1,000,000	$1,000,000
Loan to Value Ratio (LTV)	0%	60%	80%
Loan Amount	$0	$600,000	$800,000
Interest Rate	0%	7%	7%
Amortization	0 years	25 years	25 years
Annual Debt Service (ADS)	$0	$50,593	$67,457
Cash Flow (CF)	$90,000	$39,407	$22,543
Down Payment	$1,000,000	$400,000	$200,000
Cash on Cash Return	9%	9.9%	11.3%
1st Year Principal Reduction	$0	$8,874	$11,832
Return from Principal Reduction		2.2%	5.9%
Appreciation at 1%	$10,000	$10,000	$10,000
Return from Appreciation	1%	2.5%	5%
Total Annual Return	10%	14.6%	22.2%

Moderate leverage involves borrowing no more than

60% of a property's value. Many conservative financial institutions stuck to prudent lending guidelines through the last boom and didn't loan much beyond 70%, with 75% being their maximum leverage. Those that stuck to their tried-and-true lending practices continued to do well during the bust—and continued lending when other lenders retrenched or dropped from sight altogether.

As this chapter is being written, the pendulum in leverage has swung strongly to the conservative side. Now, many lenders are loaning only 60% to 70% of a property's value. Of course, the most conservative way to go is not to be leveraged at all; pay all cash and have no debt. The risk is low, but the return on investment actually decreases as well. Look at the chart again. The return in the 80% leverage scenario is double the return from the all-cash transaction.

How can this be? The chart on the next page, The Magic of Real Estate Leverage, will explain this in more detail. One of the amazing secrets of real estate investing is how leverage and time work together to grow an investor's initial capital.

There are four key components to return on investment capital. First, there is the annual cash flow generated by the property. The investor collects rent, pays the mortgage and expenses, and hopefully has cash flow left over. That cash flow is divided by the initial investment to determine the percentage return an investor will receive on his cash invested. That percentage is referred to as the investor's cash on cash return.

Second, the principal amount of the mortgage is paid down over time, which means the investor gains a greater amount of equity in the property. When the property is sold, the investor will recapture this equity, which produces a second return on investment.

Third, Appreciation is not necessarily a given with real estate investing as we have seen with the decline in property values in the last few years. But over long periods of time through up and down cycles in the market most properties historically enjoy appreciation in value.

Finally, there is a tax benefit that accrues for the investor. Years ago, the tax benefits to investing were much greater than they are today, but depreciation and the deduction of interest paid will shelter a portion of the property's income from taxation. I haven't included tax benefits in this example, but it's good to keep them in mind.

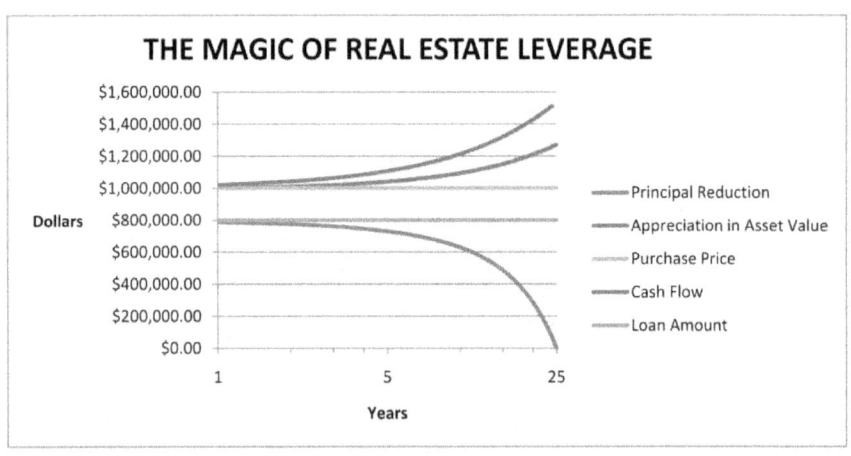

Note: This graph demonstrates the concept of principal reduction. The actual principal reduction increases exponentially toward the end of the amortization period.

Total Amount Originally Invested (Down Payment) $200,000

Total Value after 25 years (original price + appreciation + cash flow) $1,533,892

As you can see, over the 25-year projection, the

investor's initial investment of $200,000 grows to the amazing value of more than $1.5 million. This assumes appreciation of 1% annually and it doesn't take into account that there will be costs when the investor sells. But this is a realistic example that demonstrates how successful real estate investors generate vast amounts of wealth over time.

So, another key to successful real estate investing is to take on a manageable amount of debt and use leverage to increase the return on your initial investment. This amount or percentage will vary depending on a person's goals and overall financial situation. As we have seen very clearly in the recession of 2008 to 2012, real estate cycles have up years and down years. A prudent real estate investor does not allow himself to be over leveraged and risk losing his hard-earned invested capital. High leverage is usually high risk and low leverage is usually low risk. Examine the chart and determine a prudent amount of leverage that will position you to meet your investment goals.

When you combine ignorance and leverage,
you get some pretty interesting results.
Warren Buffett

~ Notes ~

~ 27 ~
Real Estate Returns Rock!

My goal is to make these real estate investment concepts simple and easy to understand. Let's compare the types of returns we should get in real estate with other investment options that are available to us. There are many places you can invest your money, but let's assume that you have $10,000 from which you want to generate a return.

First, you will determine your risk tolerance; then, you will weigh the different investment options available. On the low end of the risk scale are bank certificates of deposit. Right now, banks are paying 1–2% interest on CDs, which is not a very high return. Those are one option; bonds are another option. Bonds are rated by different risk levels. The lower the risk levels the lower the returns. The higher the risk levels the higher the returns. Today you can earn a return of 4–6% on low risk bonds.

Mutual funds may be the next option to consider. When I was a young investor, most investors felt they could get an average annual return of 10–12% on mutual funds invested in growth stocks over ten years or more. There are of course many types of mutual funds with varying degrees of risk. But just for comparison's sake let's weigh real estate investing against these investment options.

Real estate takes more time and has a greater risk

factor in some respects than CDs, bonds, and mutual funds. Naturally, as an investor you should expect to achieve a higher overall rate of return in exchange for that extra time and risk. There are the benefits that we will talk about more in this book, but there are also cash on cash returns, as well as returns that come from paying down your mortgage and from appreciation. All of these will add up over time to provide an excellent return on investment for you.

For now let's focus on the cash on cash return. I can remember a time in the eighties when demand for investment real estate far exceeded the supply. Investors from Seattle flocked to Spokane and bid property prices up so high, they were lucky to have any cash flow after making down payments as high as 30% of the purchase price. That did not make good sense. We will cover this further but keep this concept in mind: *"Buy in bad times on good economics and sell in good times on bad economics."* Those investors were buying on bad economics.

My general rule of thumb is that if you put 20–30% down on a property and have real numbers, you should be able to get a return on your cash of 5–8%. Keep in mind that times change and this is based on the current economic situation. You can't put your hard earned cash into a property and not get a reasonable return. With prime properties there is sometimes what I call a "cost of entry." In other words, you may have to pay a premium to get a high quality property that you know will produce solid, long-term returns. Maybe you stretch and there is a nominal return the first year, but by the second year you may get the 5–8% cash on cash return we talked about.

Another investing rule is to not pay more for a property than it would cost to replace it with new construction. There are exceptions to all rules, and the exception here would be if you get a mortgage that amortizes in a short period of time, such as ten years. In this case you will probably use all of your net operating income (NOI) to pay off the mortgage. There will be no cash flow. You would probably consider this only if you have a solid-credit tenant on a long-term lease and you do not anticipate any vacancy over the ten years of the mortgage. This might be an option someone retiring in ten years would consider. They do not need the income now and want to retire with no debt. Under those circumstances, if the rent will pay off the mortgage in ten years, this may be a good option for the investor.

As is noted on the Leverage Comparison chart in Chapter 26, the cash on cash return is just one component of your overall return from a real estate investment. There is also the return that comes from paying down the mortgage over time. This can amount to another 3–4% return on your cash invested. Appreciation is another component of your return. If the property goes up in value an average of just 1% per year, this component can add another 2–3% to your overall return.

There are some tax benefits generated by the interest and depreciation deductions you receive from owning the property that create an additional return. This amount is not as large as it once was but it will improve the overall return picture. It usually boils down to reducing the amount of income from the property that is taxable in the first three to six years of your investment.

Add all of these up and over a holding period of ten years or more, your overall return on investment should be between 10–14%. Many companies who arrange large, publicly traded real estate investment partnerships say that their goal is to produce an 18–20% annual rate of return for their investors.

I have been fortunate over the years to sell a few properties that generated returns from 18–21%. It is possible! Time and real estate do amazing things together—over the long haul.

As you do your homework and consider real estate investment options, work to structure your purchases to achieve these kinds of returns. The time, effort and risk you take justify a return on investment that is greater than the options available to you in stocks and bonds.

As you can imagine, with returns like I've described in this chapter, it is possible to build substantial net worth over time!

Take a chance! All life is a chance. The man who goes farthest is generally the one who is willing to do and dare.
                                              Dale Carnegie

~ 28 ~
Demographics, Visibility, and Access

An old adage states that three things matter in real estate: location, location, and location. Taking a closer look at what that really means, you might tweak the saying a bit to read, "demographics, visibility, and access." In other words, you want lots of people living and working near your property who have lots of money to spend, and they need to be able to see your property and get to it easily.

The better the demographics, usually the more valuable your property will be. More specifically, the more people with money who are within a short distance of a property, the more valuable the property is.

Successful retail companies have the study of demographics down to a science. Grocery store chains, for example, use census information, retail sales tax reports and other public information to determine how many dollars each household has available to spend on groceries in a certain geographic area. If competitors already have stores in the area, the supermarket company can estimate how many dollars for groceries are spent at each existing store—and how much potential is in that neighborhood for a new supermarket.

When looking at a specific neighborhood, density is a key criterion. Typically, a strong population density brings a high traffic count. Cities and counties count the number of cars driving on streets and calculate the average per-day traffic. Most local governments create traffic count maps and data regarding how many cars pass a property on a given day. This is important information for analyzing an investment property.

Two other key factors are exposure and access. The more visible a property is, the more attractive it will be to quality tenants. Key intersections with traffic lights measure at the top of the priority list for many national retail tenants; it's good to have a lot of cars stopped at a red light in front of your property. For example, Walgreens will only locate at high traffic, four-way lighted intersections. They will pay big money for those locations because they generate higher retails sales volumes than secondary locations.

Of course, those cars, and the potential customers who drive them, have to be able to get to your property as well—access is a key ingredient in value that can outweigh all others.

A number of years ago, I had a client who lived in the Northwest and owned a Denny's restaurant building in Des Moines, Iowa. I told him I was going to Iowa to visit family, and he asked me to drive by his property to get a feel for what he should do with it. He had constructed the building next to the on-ramp of a major interstate and signed Denny's to a long-term lease.

At the time of construction this was both a high-traffic, highly visible location with excellent access. Things went well for many years, but at some point, traffic management became an issue, and a median was installed in the street in front of Denny's. This severely limited customer access, and Denny's closed the store leaving the building vacant. The dramatic change in access turned this once-profitable real estate investment into a very challenging property, despite its robust demographics, excellent exposure and high traffic counts.

From a little different perspective, if you are investing in industrial buildings there will be a slightly different set of criteria to consider. Industrial users want access to freeways and good roads. Some industrial users need rail access to send or receive goods and materials. Access to power is another important consideration. In Washington State, some manufacturers are attracted to the low-cost hydroelectric power available. In fact, Grant County, Washington, has the lowest electrical power rates in the United States, and has become a hub for companies such as General Dynamics, Yahoo, Microsoft and BMW. Demographics are a high-priority component as well, because such industrial, warehousing and manufacturing tenants need access to an available labor force.

One reason that property values are so high in California is the high population densities of many communities. High densities equal a high demand for goods and services. Retail and business tenants want to be where the customers are. Office tenants want to be where their employees and customers live.

As you consider investment properties, take time to carefully study the demographics, visibility and access of each one. All three of these elements can have a long term impact on property values. And always remember: location, location, location!

Buy on the fringe and wait. Buy land near a growing city!
Buy real estate when other people want to sell. Hold what
you buy!

John Jacob Astor

~ 29 ~
Parking Is King!

Parking is a key ingredient for a profitable, long-term commercial real estate investment. If a building doesn't have adequate parking, it can be difficult to attract and retain good tenants. Put another way, if parking at a property is limited, the types of businesses that can successfully operate in that building are going to be limited. This is true regardless of whether you invest in office buildings, retail properties or warehouse structures.

It's really just common sense: if finding a parking place is a hassle for your tenant's customers, they will get frustrated and go to another business where the parking is easier. While parking for retail tenants and their customers is imperative, the need for employee parking is equally as important. If a business can't provide adequate parking for its employees, that business won't be interested in renting space or staying in your building.

But what about downtown areas where many buildings don't have on-site parking? The same rules essentially apply, but what becomes more important is the standard in each city. Are there ample parking garages and/or public transportation for employees and customers? In large metropolitan areas paying for parking is expected. Employees and customers know how to find parking and they are accustomed to paying for parking. My youngest daughter lives in downtown Seattle. She does not need to worry about parking because she can walk to work and shopping. Just as she has, employees and customers will adapt differently to each community's parking situation. Determine the standard in your community, and then analyze the specific parking needs of each property accordingly.

City and county governments include parking space requirements in many zoning ordinances. Oftentimes, they require a certain number of parking spaces for every 1,000 square feet of floor space a building contains. Do some research to determine how much parking is required for the different types of businesses that will potentially be renting from you. Keep in mind too, that some tenants will require more parking than the minimum amounts called for in local codes.

If you are careful, you can find lucrative opportunities investing in buildings with limited parking. You must buy the properties at the right price and know how to find a unique tenant that doesn't need standard parking. For example, there is a building on a main arterial in Spokane that is situated across from our local sports and events arena. It is a prime location but the property doesn't have any on-site parking. The last time the building was for sale, it sat on the market for a long time, and the price was reduced several times. The building's lack of parking made it virtually unusable for most buyers or tenants. As the price continued to go down, the property became a bargain opportunity for someone who could figure out a use for it. Finally, a nonprofit organization that assists blind people bought the building at an unbelievably low price. Obviously, none of the nonprofit's constituents needed parking, and the city bus stop just outside the front door made it an ideal location for their needs.

Through the years, I have purchased a couple of properties at bargain prices because they didn't have adequate parking. Again, the trick is to figure out what type of tenants can use those buildings. One of the properties I purchased was close to our local hospitals. My partners and I leased the building to one of the hospitals for records storage. We had the tenant in hand when we purchased the building. These types of deals are an exception to the rule. I wouldn't advise you to buy buildings without adequate parking unless you already know who you are going to lease the property to.

Typically, I look for buildings with an above-average number of parking spaces, because they tend to command higher rents and lease up more quickly when they become vacant. For example, I own a 5,000-square-foot office building in an attractive location at the edge of downtown Spokane. The code requirement for parking in that neighborhood is four parking spaces per 1,000 square feet of building area. That works out to 20 slots for a 5,000-square-foot building like mine. Fortunately, my property has 32 parking spaces, which gives the property a big advantage over neighboring buildings when we are competing for new tenants.

What's the bottom line here? Parking is a key ingredient to a profitable real estate investment. You can never have an overabundance of it.

Buy land. They ain't making any more of the stuff.
Will Rogers

~ Notes ~

~ 30 ~
Property Management

Early in your investing career, you'll probably need to do what I did: manage both the investment partnerships you form *and* the properties you buy. This will be a very valuable learning experience. You will learn quickly that overseeing your investment property and partnerships takes time. If you're like me, though, it won't be long before you realize you can't do it all on your own, especially if you still have a day job! Eventually, you will either need to hire someone to assist you or hire a professional property management firm.

Like many occupations, property management takes a special set of skills, education and experience. A property manager must be well-versed on all aspects of working with tenants and taking care of a property, including being knowledgeable on landlord-tenant laws. Their duties include contracting for and overseeing repairs and routine maintenance, collecting rents, paying bills and keeping accurate records. It is also necessary as a property manager to have an assertive and firm personality. This is essential for dealing effectively with problem tenants and other issues that arise. Some of us have those personality skills and some of us don't. We do need to be cordial and diplomatic but there are many occasions when we need to take a firm stand on issues or it ends up costing us a lot of time and money.

Throughout my career, I have encountered many

property owners who lacked the personality and skills necessary to manage their properties themselves. At one time, I did some leasing work for an elderly widow who owned a number of properties that she and her husband had acquired over many years. Her husband had been a very effective manager of those properties while he was alive. Prior to his death he told his wife that she should never sell any of their properties. This was good advice; all of the properties were debt free, and many of them were well built brick buildings in quality locations. These properties produced a comfortable retirement income for this couple.

After her husband's death the widow continued to manage the properties by herself. As the years passed, though, the widow became friends with some of her tenants and, as a result, she was reluctant to raise their rents. Her operating costs increased over time to the point that they ate up a large portion of her income from the properties. When vacancies popped up, she was so stringent about the kind of tenants she would allow in her properties that spaces ended up sitting empty for many years. If she had hired a good property manager, her investment portfolio would have stood a better chance of maintaining the high level of profitability that it had before her husband died.

As you can see from this unfortunate example, it's important to do an honest self assessment of your business and management skills. Are you well suited to the task or would you be better off hiring a professional property manager to take care of your properties? Again, the amount of time you have available is important as well. It's possible that you or a family member have time to learn the ins and outs of the property management business. And, if you are buying a property without partners and have a building with a single tenant, it makes managing it yourself that much easier. However, the more people involved—tenants and partners—the more complex it can become to manage your properties effectively.

As my real estate portfolio has grown, I've found that hiring good property managers has given me tremendous leverage of my time. Now, I oversee the work done by the property managers and review the monthly financial statements from my properties.

Before hiring a property manager, make sure you use some of the same skills you use when doing your due diligence on a real estate acquisition. Talk with other property owners to get input on the property-management firms in your community. Find a firm that specializes in managing the types of properties you own. Drive by the properties they manage; get out of the car and look at them. Are they well cared for? Would you be happy with the appearance of the properties? Talk to the tenants and get their input on the management and care of the property. Are the property managers responsive and polite?

A professional property manager can greatly enhance the financial operation of a property. Large property management firms have bulk buying power and can contract, in many instances, for supplies and services less expensively than an individual can. Again, carefully consider the value of your time. If your time is worth $100 an hour, should you be doing $25- or $35-per-hour tasks?

Weigh your options carefully. The profitability of your

investment depends on it and you will sleep better at night.

Landlords grow rich in their sleep.
John Stewart Mill

~ 31 ~
Tenant Improvements

Fasten your seat belts! We are going into a little more detail with the topic of tenant improvements. They are a very important component of real estate investing and require the careful investment of additional capital in your property. Tenant improvements (TIs) are necessary to attract and retain good tenants in most types of investment real estate. The amount and type of improvements required by a new or renewing tenant will vary for office, retail and industrial properties. They will also vary depending on the established norms and market conditions in your community.

In this chapter we will focus on the TIs needed for office buildings, as they are usually the most TI-intensive type of investment real estate. As you learn how to manage the TI process for an office building, the skills you gain will be transferrable to any type of investment real estate. Before we talk about office building TIs, let's address the importance of a property's first impressions.

First and foremost, in order to attract tenants to your building, you must have strong exterior curb appeal. When a prospective tenant drives up to the building, a well-manicured parking lot, landscaping and overall exterior should compel them to proceed inside. As they enter the building, the common areas should also be well kept and attractive. All of your available interior spaces must be ready to lease and in the most marketable condition possible. You would be surprised by how often this basic, crucial component of real estate investing and managing gets overlooked.

Moving to the interior, let's discuss the TIs needed for most small office building tenants. When a tenant moves out of a small generic office space, which in our market is less than 2,000 square feet, it is usually sufficient to clean the carpet and paint the walls in order to attract and meet the needs of a new tenant. If the former tenant had occupied the space for many years, you may also need to install new carpet and replace ceiling tiles. Two by four standard acoustical ceiling tiles can get dirty and chipped over the years. They can be cleaned or painted, but eventually they should to be replaced to look fresh and attractive to a new tenant. It is important to have your vacant space in top shape and ready to lease because many smaller tenants want to look at just a few spaces, pick one that fits their needs, sign a lease and move in. They may not want to wait for the time it takes for the space to be cleaned up or renovated.

The needs of larger office tenants (occupying over 2,000 square feet) tend to be unique to the nature of their business. So, those tenants will likely request that you provide them with new TIs or modifications to the existing improvements as a part of their lease agreement. A preliminary design of those improvements is called a **space plan**. Prospective tenants will need a space plan so they can see how their business will fit into the space you have for lease. The space plan will also be used to determine the estimated cost of the improvements needed by the tenant. Because tenants will expect you to design a space for them and provide them with a market amount of TIs, having a qualified architect or space planner in your tool kit is essential.

I use a couple of low overhead and low cost small architectural firms to do most of my general day to day space planning for small tenants. When I am working with a larger, more sophisticated tenant, I hire a space planner or architect with the experience and expertise to work effectively with that tenant. As an example, if we are working to lease a medical office building, then we hire a space planner who is experienced in working with medical office space users. Incidentally, it is wise with larger projects to give tenants an allowance for space planning. If you don't, some may plan excessively and run up a large architectural bill at great cost to you.

Another option is to have the contractor provide ***preliminary*** space plans for prospective tenants. Many contractors are skilled at using space planning software and will provide this service for you at no cost if they know you will use them for the construction of the improvements. Once basic space plans are agreed to, the contractor can give them to your architect to finalize.

It is important to help tenants envision how the space will work for their business and how it will look once construction is complete. If you have other space in the building or another building nearby with recently built out space you can use that as an example to show the tenant the type of improvements you would provide for them. You can also utilize an interior decorator that will provide a color board showing carpet samples, finish materials and paint colors that are available for the tenant to choose from.

Many years ago an investor friend named Pat called me. He owned a single tenant office building in downtown Spokane which had been vacant for about two years. Pat asked me to tour the property and advise him on how to get the space leased. I met him at the property and we walked around the interior of the building. It was about 3,000 square feet and had an open floor plan, except for a couple of offices and bathrooms located against the back wall of the structure. Right away, it was obvious to me why no one had been interested in leasing Pat's building. It had dark wood paneling and orange shag carpet from the 1970s, and this was the late 1980s! All he needed was to install new carpet, get rid of the dark paneling and repaint the walls a light color. I assured Pat that with those improvements in place, the building would lease out in no time.

Sure enough, as soon as the work was done, Pat was able to secure a lease with a great tenant. Was he taking a risk by putting in the new carpet, not knowing if a tenant would need other improvements? Not really. The interior was mostly open space, so if additional offices were needed the new walls could be installed right over the top of the new carpet. As with Pat's building, sometimes existing, outdated improvements create an obstacle to securing a new tenant. When this is the case it is best to remove all of the old improvements—including the floor covering—and have a clean, wide open space to show a potential client.

Prior to the current recession, landlords in downtown Spokane commonly offered prospective tenants improvement allowances of $20 to $25 per square foot and required them to pay any costs above that amount. Today, due to a very soft office leasing market, motivated landlords must provide most or all of the TIs requested by tenants in order to complete any deals. The current cost to demolish the old and build out new improvements in an office building is around $30 to $35 per useable square foot of space occupied. So, the cost for an owner to build out space for a 3,000 square foot tenant is $90,000 to $105,000. As the economy improves and the office market recovers, the scales will tip back to where landlords will not have to provide as many incentives to attract tenants.

When making a substantial investment in TIs, it is important to ensure that your prospective tenant has a viable business and good credit. Sometimes however, even when a tenant appears to be solid financially, unexpected setbacks do happen. Several years ago I arranged a lease with a businessman named Chuck, for part of a new office building my partners and I had built. I had known Chuck for many years and watched his telecommunications business grow from a small, one-man operation to a very successful enterprise. He had outgrown his existing space and our building fit his needs very well. We negotiated a lease and agreed to provide him with the TIs he needed for the 3,000 square feet of office space his company would occupy. The lease was signed and my contractor partner built out the space for Chuck.

About the time Chuck was supposed to move into our building, his company lost their largest client. As a result, he said that he would not be able to move into our building. Not only that, he would probably have to close down his business altogether. This put my partners and me in a tough situation, but eventually, we found another tenant who was able to utilize the improvements we had built out for Chuck. That was a good outcome from an unforeseen challenge. Even though a measure of risk is always there, you mitigate the risk by making sure you get a credit report, financial statements and learn as much as you can about each tenant before finalizing a lease.

Another strong recommendation is that you carefully consider the type of TIs requested by your tenant. If the TIs are unusual or specific to their business and cannot be used by a future tenant, then require them to pay for the improvements they are requesting. For instance, a tenant once asked us to build a special sound proof room for anger management counseling. The sound proofing was very expensive and we doubted that any future tenant could benefit from such an amenity, so we required the tenant to pay the extra costs associated with the room. Each situation is different, and with every tenant you need to carefully consider what improvements you will or will not provide for them. Having an experienced TI contractor or broker to assist you with these decisions is crucial.

When it comes to hiring a contractor to do TIs there is an old saying that goes, "You don't hire General Motors to build a wheel barrow". It is important to find a TI contractor that fits the scale of the work you need done. For small construction jobs, look for a small contractor who fits that scale. Many small contractors specialize in TI jobs and, because their own staff can do much of the work, they are very cost effective. If you have a major construction job, consider a larger contractor who has the skills and breadth of experience to handle that type of project.

Early in my career as a broker, I negotiated a lease for a marketing company that was selling some of the first timeshare vacation condominiums in the United States. We worked out the terms of a lease with a building owner, subject to the owner's broker getting a satisfactory bid to build out the needed improvements. The owner of the building was from out of town and requested that his broker get two bids from large, reputable construction companies. He wanted a contractor that was well known and dependable since he would have to oversee the project remotely.

The two bids obtained by his broker came in at $28,900 and $31,500. Based on the rent we had agreed to for the lease, the owner of the building could not justify the cost of the improvements. He said the tenant would have to pay part of the bill or he would not go forward with the lease. I was eager to finalize the deal, so I asked Charlie, a senior broker in my office at the time, how to overcome this impasse. He referred me to Stan, a small contractor who worked from his home. Since he had no office and he did most of the work himself (with the help of a couple of hired hands), Stan had very low overhead which enabled him to submit an astounding low bid at $22,750! With this new estimate in hand, I went back to the broker representing the owner, and we completed the lease to everyone's satisfaction.

I learned a number of valuable lessons from that experience. First, as noted earlier, you really don't "hire General Motors to build a wheel barrow". In other words, pick the right sized contractor for the work you need done. Second, it pays to shop around and be creative in looking for construction solutions. I have worked with a variety of trustworthy, well known contractors for many years, and I hire them based on the size and type of job I need done. Even so, with many positive, long term contractor relationships, I keep my eye out for young, up and coming contractors. Things change over time, people retire, and it is good to be open to new business opportunities.

There are a couple of ways to hire a contractor to do TI work for you: getting bids or negotiating a **cost plus** contract. I have done both with equal success. When you solicit bids for TIs, contractors bid the job and provide you with a guaranteed price for which they will complete the project. Then they do the work and manage the project to cover their costs and make a profit. It is very important to have a reputable contractor who will do quality work and treat you fairly. If the contractor is assuming all the risk, you do not want him taking shortcuts to ensure his profit from the job—especially if he underbid the job and knows that he is going to break even or lose money.

Since all of the contractors I work with are people I know with a lot of experience, I usually select the contractor with the lowest bid. There are times, however, when I do *not* select the low bidder. Maybe a certain contractor has more experience working in a certain building and knows its unique characteristics better than anyone else. He may end up doing a better job for slightly more money than the low bidder. Or, he may recommend some cost saving ideas based on his intimate knowledge of the building. Having a contractor you know and trust minimizes the opportunity for "surprises" that can come up during the construction process.

I also have a select group of contractors that I work

with on a **cost plus** basis. With cost plus, I select the best contractor to fit the job and then negotiate a fee for them to do the work for me. They solicit bids from multiple subcontractors and select the best sub bids. They manage the construction job and give me a copy of all their subcontractor invoices so I know exactly what everything cost. I then pay the contractor the agreed-to fee on top of the exact costs of the job. I have done this with TI and construction jobs of all sizes.

The fee I pay the contractor will vary depending on the size of the job and can be a percentage or a flat amount. On most small jobs I pay contractors cost plus a fee of around 8 to 12%. The percentage usually goes down as the job gets larger. In addition to their fee (or profit), some contractors ask for an overhead cost associated with the project, which might pay for office and insurance costs, or even a project supervisor if the contractor is not doing the supervision himself. The overhead amount can be negotiated as well. As with TIs, fees and contractor agreements will vary from market to market throughout the United States.

There is both a benefit and a risk to doing work on a cost plus basis. The benefit is that if there are any savings in the project, they will accrue to you. The contractor will provide you with cost estimates and bids from multiple subcontractors before you start so you should have a good handle on your costs. The risk is that you take on the cost of any unknowns that come along in the project.

So, in addition to having a good contractor you need to be able to assume the risk of unexpected costs that can occur during construction. It is not an exact science, especially if you are working in an existing building.

Unforeseen issues almost always arise; you never know what will or will not be behind the walls! So to minimize the risk of the unknowns, every project should have a contingency fund that will cover such expenses. It would not be unreasonable to have a contingency equal to 10% of the project cost. Of course, this amount can be adjusted based on each individual project and as you gain experience in the construction process.

Sometimes it is also prudent to negotiate a late fee or penalty with your contractor. If their work is not done by an agreed upon date, then there is a daily penalty that gets deduced from your cost until the work is done. Many times, you are obligated to deliver space to a tenant by a certain date, and you need to know that you can meet your deadline. Many tenants will negotiate to include language in the lease agreement that allows them to terminate if the space is not available by a certain date. Keep this in mind as you work with your TI contractor.

Once you begin work, it is common for a tenant to inspect the progress of construction and request changes or additions to what was originally agreed upon. These additions are usually referred to as **change orders**. For this reason, it is important to spell out in your lease how you will deal with any such requests by the tenant during the course of construction. The lease should clearly state that after the landlord and tenant have agreed to the project specifications and plans, any and all changes made at the request of the tenant will be at their expense. This needs to be clearly communicated to the contractor as well.

I recall a situation where a landlord hired a contractor

to build TIs for a national tenant to whom he had leased space. During the construction process, the local manager for the company leasing the space requested many changes to the work being done by the contractor. The contractor made the changes and they were billed to the owner at the end of the job. A dispute arose over who was responsible for the change orders. Due to a construction contract that provided for all change orders made by the landlord or the tenant to be paid by the landlord, plus a poorly worded lease, the landlord ended up paying for the extra improvements. So it is important to clarify in the lease which party is responsible for change orders, and to stay involved in the day to day construction process. If you know what is going on it is easier to respond to issues as they arise.

You may be wondering how most investors come up with the money needed for TIs. Hopefully the investors have set aside a cash reserve to cover some or all of the costs. If not, they may need to get a bank loan based on a new lease with the tenant or refinance their existing mortgage on the building. In a worst case scenario, there is a cash call and the investment partners chip in for the costs from personal funds. There are many ways to finance improvements in your building. It's up to you as you consider owning a building, to carefully plan so that you can pay for the TIs that will inevitably be needed over the life of your investment.

As you can see, understanding and managing office building TIs requires a certain degree of knowledge and experience. As in any new endeavor, with study and patience you can learn the tricks of the trade and become proficient and successful. So carefully consider the long-

and short-term TIs needed for any property you are planning to invest in. You'll want to determine how the cost of those improvements will affect your long-term return on investment. Then, develop a good team of construction professionals to work with so that the TI design and construction process for your properties is efficient, cost effective, and profitable!

Ninety percent of all millionaires become so through owning real estate.
Andrew Carnegie

~ 32 ~
The Paperwork

There are many very important legal documents you will deal with regularly as a real estate investor. It is important to get to know these documents intimately. In some respects you will need to become a layman attorney as it relates to the real estate paperwork. You must learn to understand these documents—and the language in them—in great detail. With time and study you can master the finer points and hire an attorney when it is appropriate. Don't get me wrong here; I am not under playing the role of a good real estate attorney. A good attorney who specializes in real estate must become part of your investment strategy. But even with an attorney on your team, you must have a clear grasp of the legal documents related to real estate to be a successful investor.

I have worked with many excellent real estate attorneys over the years. I have found several who are highly skilled with documents and document language. Other attorneys are capable of representing you well if you have an issue that requires court action (Of course, staying out of court is always the best course of action!). Some attorneys are proficient at both document management and legal representation. Make sure you search carefully and choose an attorney who fits your needs as a real estate investor.

Let's look at the two most common documents that a real estate investor deals with. The first is the **real estate purchase and sale agreement**. Whenever you make an offer to purchase property, you will use a purchase and sale agreement. This should be a comprehensive agreement put together by an attorney, legal document company or real estate organization. The language of the agreement should fit the laws of the state in which you are purchasing real estate. There are generic documents that will work in multiple states but it is best to have a document that fits the state you are in. The language in a purchase and sale agreement is most important when a problem arises; in such a situation you want to be protected and have a legally binding document.

In Washington State the Commercial Brokers Association (CBA) has engaged attorneys over the years to provide their brokers with an updated set of forms that comply with the laws of the state of Washington. They are excellent documents and protect the parties involved.

Here are a few important points to keep in mind as a buyer of investment real estate:

- Make sure that you have the correct legal entities listed on the document.
- Make sure you have the legal description of the property correct and completely spelled out.
- Make sure that you have a very clear contingency clause (due diligence) that gives you a time period to inspect the property and determine if you want to purchase it. That clause must allow you to cancel

the transaction and receive a full refund of your earnest money if for any reason you are not satisfied with the property during the due diligence period.

- If possible use earnest money in the form of a note due if and when you remove your contingencies. This saves you from putting up cash that will sit in a trust account for a property you may not purchase.
- Request that the seller provide and pay for a current Phase I Environmental Report upon acceptance of your purchase and sale agreement. If the seller will not pay for a Phase I, pay for one yourself. You can ask the seller to reimburse you for the report if it shows that the property has contamination and you want to cancel the transaction.
- Make sure that the purchase and sale agreement allows you to assign the agreement to another entity.
- Read the default language in the agreement carefully. In the event of default, you want the seller's only remedy to be limited to retaining your earnest money. Default would occur if you remove your contingencies, put up your earnest money, agree to close, and then change your mind and do not close.
- Make sure all hand written changes made to the purchase and sale agreement during negotiation are initialed and dated. These agreements can get a little messy with a lot of back and forth negotiation.

All parties want to be very clear on what their final agreement is. When the changes to the agreement are not legible it can cause problems.

- Remember that you can never be too specific. Tie down all the details. If you think something is not clear, clarify it.
- Request that the seller provide you with a preliminary title report upon acceptance of your offer; then, read the title report. Look for any easements, agreements or other issues that may affect the property.

The next document that you will need to be familiar with is a **lease**. I could write a whole book on leases and lease clauses. Our goal in this book is to cover all the key concepts in real estate investing so we will just touch on the highlights of leases. Make sure you find a current lease document that adequately protects you as the investor and property owner. See Appendix C, Additional Resources, for websites where you can find samples of lease documents.

Leases have gotten much more complex over the years and it is now common for landlords to engage an attorney to work out the lease language issues brought up by prospective tenants and their legal counsel. I am not talking about deal points, just lease language. Insurance language in leases can be very complicated.

When I first started my real estate investing career I used a lease that took up both sides of two sheets of legal paper. Those were the good old days! Today I use a multi-page lease, and have actually worked with leases as long as one hundred pages. Now that is a bit much. Here are some key points to be aware of when it comes to leases:

- When purchasing an investment property with leases in place, READ ALL THE LEASES! If the copies you receive are not legible or complete, get copies that are. This is an area where huge mistakes are made.
- When entering into a lease with a tenant, make sure that you have the correct legal description of the property and the correct legal name or names of the parties to whom you are leasing.
- Obtain a credit report on every tenant you are considering.
- If tenant improvements are being done to the space the tenant is occupying, spell out very specifically what improvements are being done and who is responsible for paying for them.
- In Washington State, on leases of one year or more, a lease is not valid unless the signature of the landlord is notarized. Check your state laws and act accordingly.
- Always have a late fee in your lease that will deter late payment of rent and compensate you in the event the tenant does pay late.
- This will vary by market and demand, but work to include a deposit or last month's rent in addition to the first month's rent when the lease is signed.
- This applies to all legal agreements, but again you can never be too specific: Make sure that all the responsibilities of the parties are clearly spelled out in writing.

That is a very quick overview of "the paperwork." Read

purchase and sale agreements and leases and study the meaning of each paragraph. Take classes on understanding and working with these documents. A thorough understanding of these documents is essential to your success as a real estate investor.

He who is his own lawyer has a fool for a client.
Author unknown

A lawyer's time and advice is his stock and trade.
Abraham Lincoln

~ 33 ~
How to Get And Keep Good Tenants

We've talked a lot about picking the right real estate investment property. Now, let's talk about another important component: selecting good tenants.

Good tenants pay their rent on time and live up to their obligations under the lease. In doing so, they also substantially reduce the time and effort it takes to manage a property. Most importantly, they help you pay off your mortgages and provide you with a return on your investment.

How do you go about finding good tenants? The most obvious step is to hire a good commercial leasing agent. As I've mentioned, I rely on leasing agents to find most of the tenants for my properties. A quality agent who is dedicated to finding good tenants is invaluable.

Additionally, I'm always on the lookout for potential tenants as I'm going about my day-to-day business. I talk with owners of the businesses I frequent and find out how their current location is working for them. My goal is to establish relationships with all the business owners I meet and find out more about their long-term real estate needs.

For example, my wife and I work out together after lunch once a week. We have found through the years that we have a better workout if we have something to eat first, so we share a sandwich at a locally owned sandwich shop near our gym. Over time, we have gotten to know the sandwich shop owner, Judy, and she confided to me recently that her lease was coming up in a couple of years. She also said that she wasn't pleased with the gentleman who managed the property she was leasing. I have a space in mind for her, and I hope to offer her a better location when her lease expires. Judy has been in business for 17 years and has five locations. She is the type of stable tenant with whom any building owner would love to have a leasing relationship.

Of course, you aren't always going to know as much about a prospective tenant as I know about Judy. Picking a good tenant is just like any other prudent decision-making process. It's wise to gather as much information as you can and analyze that information carefully to make an informed decision. Specifically, you need to find out as much about the tenant's business history as possible. If the business is new, find out as much as you can about the owner's personal and employment history. I always request a personal financial statement from prospective tenants and obtain a credit report on them. Sometimes I have also asked for two or three years of federal income tax returns. If the business is new, I will ask for personal and banking references—and, I will follow up and call those references.

My track record for selecting tenants is relatively good, but I've also learned some valuable lessons the hard way.

If a tenant is in a big hurry to get moved into your building, proceed with caution. More often than not, I have found such a sense of urgency to be a red flag. I have been burned a couple of times by tenants who were in a hurry to get out of their existing space because of a dispute with their current landlord or because they were way behind in rent. Again, be especially cautious if a tenant is in a hurry to get into your space.

A few years ago, there was a dentist who was pretty eager to get into a building I was trying to lease. He also wanted me to spend a lot of money on tenant improvements for him. Upon reviewing his personal financial statement, it was evident that he had entirely too much debt, even though his revenues were substantial. Concerned about what I saw, I ordered a credit report. Sure enough, he had declared personal bankruptcy five years earlier. It appeared to me that he was on the road to bankruptcy again, so I politely passed on leasing space to him.

While there is often reason to be wary, a business might have a legitimate need to lease space quickly. Maybe a retailer wants a new store to open before the Christmas shopping season starts. In another case, an office tenant has been given notice by their landlord to move from their existing location because another tenant is expanding and has dibs on that space. I have made some deals with good tenants who were operating on a tight time schedule, and it has worked out just fine.

I have also found that if prospective tenants are unreasonable and difficult to deal with during lease negotiations, they will also be unreasonable and difficult throughout the life of the lease. High maintenance tenants can be a headache and they are typically the ones who have a gripe about something, get behind in their rent or move out in the middle of the night. Unless you are desperate to fill your space, you are usually better off waiting for a better tenant.

Once I have signed a lease with a tenant I will do everything I can to help them be successful. I will do business with them if I can and will encourage my friends to do so as well. If my tenants are successful, my real estate investments are successful!

But what happens when good tenants come upon hard times? Let's say the company's revenues are down, and they are struggling to pay their rent. My goal has always been to work with my tenants the best I can to help keep them in business. At times, I have reduced rent, and at other times, I have completely forgiven rent. I simply find these measures are worth it to keep good tenants, especially in weak markets.

In these challenging times, many tenants are asking for rent relief. Some need it, and some are asking just because others are doing so. Today, we ask to see such tenants' books and find out if they have a legitimate request for a rent reduction.

Over the years, I have been fortunate to develop strong relationships with many of my tenants. I cannot stress this enough: If you have good relationships with your tenants, it is a lot easier to resolve problems, such as leaky roofs and other maintenance issues. If your tenants know you care, they will often give you plenty of space to get things squared away.

A positive relationship with your tenants can help in other ways, too. Tenants who are treated well will usually stay in your building as long as their business does not out grow their space. Your tenants can also be a great reference when you are trying to attract other tenants to your building.

With most tenants if you respond to issues during their tenancy in a timely manner and treat them fairly, they will usually respond similarly. I am not saying that you need to give away the farm, just perform your obligations under the lease promptly and treat your tenants the way you would want to be treated. Then when leases come up for renewal offer your tenants market renewal terms and they will most likely continue their occupancy. Keeping your buildings full of content tenants adds a lot to your bottom line.

When successful developer Trammell Crow first started in business, he visited each of his tenants once a month. His love and concern for his tenants and their business success resulted in great loyalty. For many of these clients, he ended up constructing multiple buildings throughout the United States.

Good tenants can make life as a real estate investor very satisfying, so work hard to attract and retain them!

Love people and use money; don't use
people and love money.
Author unknown

~ Notes ~

~ 34 ~
Don't Fall In Love

Over the years, I have seen a number of people who let their emotions get in the way of making good real estate decisions. They fall in love with a building or piece of land and start thinking with their hearts instead of their heads. But know this, regardless of how pretty a building is or how promising a piece of land appears to be, love of real estate is usually an unrequited love. Try to resist becoming emotionally "invested" in your potential real estate investment, because it will never love you back.

To make sure you're thinking rationally rather than emotionally, do the math and determine two numbers once you find a property you want to consider purchasing. First, determine what you would like to pay for a property. Then, determine the maximum amount you *should* pay. Once you have set these two parameters, do your best to negotiate the purchase price somewhere between them.

Of course, this is easier said than done for some investors. Emotional decisions are made in real estate transactions every day. I have one friend who is a very successful buy-and-hold real estate investor. I asked him once if he had sold very many properties through the years. He said, "Only when someone has offered me more than the property was worth!" I can't say with absolute certainty, but I would guess many of those buyers made decisions with their hearts rather than their heads.

Of course, there is an exception to every rule. Recently, I ran into a friend, Bill, who owns an upholstery business and the building it occupies. He said he was considering buying a vacant lot adjacent to his building. The lot is small—only about 25 feet wide—and much of it is solid rock. It would be very hard to develop and tough to sell to most buyers. Because it's adjacent to his building, Bill has coveted the lot for many years and has always wanted to add parking spaces for his business there. The lot was put up for sale recently, but it's priced above what an appraiser would probably say it is worth.

If Bill were to buy the 25-foot lot and add parking spaces there for his customers, he would increase the overall value of his existing property as well as the 25-foot lot. I told him he could afford to pay top dollar for the property if his reason was attached to a wise business decision, such as adding parking spaces for his existing building and customers.

If you choose to pay top dollar for a property, make sure the reason is a good business decision and not some sort of emotional rationalization. Consider the example I gave in Chapter 22. I paid top dollar for the property, but ended up with great cash flow because of falling interest rates which eventually pushed up values on all investment real estate.

One thing I have learned in this business is that there is always another deal somewhere. If the numbers don't make sense, move on and keep looking until you find a deal where the numbers make good sense for you. Get excited about the deal and its terms—but don't get swept up in feelings for the property. I can think of many times when a buyer I knew held firm to his offer, and the seller finally got motivated enough to come back and accept the terms that were offered.

You will find plenty of outstanding properties that will be easy to get excited about. Stick to the target numbers you have set for buying the property. If you can't get a deal done at those numbers, move on. Remember, successful investors *buy in tough times on good economics and sell in good times on bad economics.*

The ability to say "no" is a tremendous advantage for an investor.
Warren Buffett

No fine work can be done without concentration and self-sacrifice and toil and doubt.
Max Beerbohm

~ Notes ~

~ 35 ~
When to Sell

If you are going to maximize your wealth-building potential, it doesn't make sense to sell property. As I said in Chapter 16, you build net worth by accumulating assets, not by disposing of them. But many people ask, shouldn't you have an exit strategy? Even with a buy-and-hold philosophy, isn't there a time to sell?

The answer is yes, but I personally think there are only a couple circumstances when an investor should consider selling.

The most obvious is when you need cash. Ideally, this would be cash needed to meet a financial goal, like paying for a child's college education or buying a vacation home. There may be times when you just need the cash. We all have to eat and we all have bills to pay. In either case, you have to weigh present needs against your long-term goals.

The second situation is when someone wants your property enough that they will pay you more than market value for it. Every once in a while you get lucky! Someone falls in love with your property and offers you a crazy price for it. Other times, a neighbor needs your property badly to expand their business and makes an above-market-value offer. When an offer you can't refuse is on the table, make sure it is high enough for you to justify paying the closing costs and income taxes.

Please note, neither of the two reasons to sell

mentioned above has anything to do with the property's performance. From time to time, everybody ends up with a real estate investment that doesn't work out as planned. The property might have some physical characteristics that result in higher-than-normal maintenance costs. The location might not be as desirable to tenants as you initially thought, or traffic patterns might shift, making it hard to keep the building leased. Any seasoned real estate investor will have property that meets one of these criteria. Regardless, I don't think underperformance is reason enough to reduce net worth by unloading a building.

One way or another, all properties can meet a need in the marketplace. I've only seen a few properties through the years that had severe enough shortcomings to justify their sale. As the saying goes, *"There is a butt for every seat."* In other words, most properties are attractive to some kind of tenant at the right price and terms. You might have to lower your anticipated rent or invest in some improvements for the property, but it's usually worth your time to keep the property and find its niche in the marketplace.

When you consider putting a property on the market, keep in mind that selling a property typically involves substantial costs that will reduce your net worth. These costs vary. In Washington State, all real estate sellers pay a state excise tax, which is almost 2% of the property's sale price. Add to that a sales commission, title insurance, and other closing costs and you've lost a substantial amount of your net worth. Once the property sells, you'll pay either ordinary income tax or long-term capital-gains tax on any profit you have in the transaction. The tax can vary, but most people under the current United States tax law will pay a minimum 15% capital gains tax. Some states may also have an income tax that could apply as well. Add up all of those costs and taxes and you could be giving up as much as 25% of your hard earned equity!

So you need to carefully examine the reasons you are selling and make sure it is really what you want to do. Is getting the cash for another investment worth the cost of selling? Does the reason for selling really justify the costs you will incur? The potential loss of net worth by selling is why many of the very successful real estate investors I know are buy-and-hold investors.

If you are selling to generate cash for a more attractive property there is the option of doing a **1031 tax-free exchange**. Under a 1031 exchange, the IRS allows you under certain guidelines to sell a property, place the proceeds with a certified exchange facilitator, and then reinvest those funds in another property. If you take a portion of the proceeds from the sale in cash, those funds are fully taxable. Otherwise, any taxable gains on the sale of the property are transferred into the tax basis of the new property. You are deferring any taxable gain into the future when you sell and take cash proceeds. This has been a very popular way to postpone paying taxes on the sale of a property. A good reference on 1031 exchanges is discussed in Gary Gorman's book *Exchanging Up*. And most facilitators also have websites with helpful information on how to effectively carry out a 1031 exchange. See Appendix C.

Yes, there will be times when you want to consider selling, but give very careful consideration to the reasons why before you move forward. I can think of one property in particular, where my partners and I experienced some cash flow issues for about two years. One of my partners grew frustrated with continually writing checks to fund our shortfalls. He suggested we just get rid of it. I encouraged him to hang in there, and eventually we got the issues with the property resolved. The cash flow has been consistent for many years now, and once we pay off our mortgage in the near future, it will produce *Cash Flow Forever.* My partner is certainly glad we didn't sell when he wanted to!

Our favorite holding period is forever.
Warren Buffett

~ 36 ~
So You Want To Be a Developer

It seems to me that nearly everybody wants to be a developer. Through the years, I have had a number of aspiring real estate investors ask me how they can get into development. Many people think that being a developer is an easy way to make big money. Successful developers can and do create substantial wealth. Commercial real estate development is, however, a profession that requires a broad range of specialized skills, a lot of cash and the ability to manage substantial risk. So it is a business where people can easily lose a lot of money if they have not mastered the required skills, or if they get caught in an unexpected down cycle in the market. I have seen many very skilled, quality developers get caught in a down market and lose a lot of money.

During a down cycle in the real estate market, understandably, less people are interested in becoming developers. However, as soon as the business climate improves and the headlines about developers going broke become less common, history eventually repeats itself. Once again, a lot of folks want to be real estate developers.

As we begin to explore real estate development, we must return to the subject of leverage. Through every down cycle, many developers have gone broke because they were highly leveraged. If you want to be a successful developer, you have to be acutely aware of your financial capacity. When times get tough—and they will get tough at some point in the cycle—you need to be prepared to weather the economic storm. That means having a lot of cash available and being able to manage the debt you take on in a worst case scenario.

If you want to read a compelling story about a developer who experienced the highest of the highs and lowest of the lows, then you will enjoy *Zeckendorf: An Autobiography of William Zeckendorf.* William Zeckendorf was a very colorful and successful New York City developer who built some of the great high-rise office buildings that define the Big Apple skyline. In the New York City development arena, there are millions of dollars at stake and long construction timeframes. Many significant changes can take place in the real estate market during the years it takes to complete such massive projects. Developers like Zeckendorf must have been gifted with amazing vision and an iron constitution to withstand the changing market forces they dealt with over the duration of such large projects.

But not every development is as monumental as the Chrysler Building. Many developers work on a smaller scale within their communities and make a good living completing quality projects. Most of them have developed a broad range of skills and have a high degree of experience. It's not a game for beginners, and I would caution anybody against getting into real estate development until they have gained a solid base of real estate investment, construction and ownership experience.

A very successful developer once told me, "*Anybody*

can try and be a developer, but very few people master the trade and make any money." He's right: real estate development is a highly specialized skill. Making money in real estate development requires a clear understanding of and skilled efficiency with each step of the development process. You create value and net worth by managing the costs at every step in the development process.

This starts with purchasing the land at the right price and knowing what unique costs will be associated with building on the property. Is the land flat or sloped? Is the soil properly compacted or solid rock? How is the property zoned, and will that affect how you can use it? What steps are required to meet local codes and requirements? What entitlements and related fees are necessary to get a building permit? As you can see, when it comes to buying land, it's actually not quite as simple as the old mantra, *location, location, location.*

Successful developers tend to specialize in one type of property. Then, they work hard to understand and figure out all the efficiencies and tricks associated with that property type to maximize profitability. With each project, they refine their skills and gain a keen understanding of each nuance of a property. Some developers build and hold projects; others develop, lease out the space, and sell at a profit.

For those who master the skills of developing property, the rewards are both personally satisfying and financially rewarding. You work to create a project that looks good, is appreciated by your tenants, and provides cash flow while you own it and a profit when you sell it. Even experienced developers have projects that don't go as planned, and the related financial stress can be, well, stressful. As I said before, it takes a tough constitution to manage the issues that accompany a complicated project.

Here is an example of a development project that was successful: Two partners and I bought a small piece of land, half of which was zoned for apartments; the other half was zoned for industrial uses. Due to the quirky zoning, we were able to buy the property for only $45,000, which worked out to $1.50 per square foot and represented a good value at the time.

The property bordered a residential neighborhood, and we met with the local neighborhood council, telling them we'd be happy to build either an apartment or industrial building on the site. Our preference was to go industrial, and many of the homeowners didn't want to live next to apartments. The neighborhood council agreed not to oppose our request to rezone the property to allow industrial development on the whole parcel.

Once we secured the proper zoning, we designed a 7,500 square-foot office and warehouse building with five 1,500 square-foot bays. Construction went smoothly, and we leased up all of the space in the building.

We owned the property for about seven years. During that time, we kept the building leased and in good condition, using any cash flow that was generated to pay down the mortgage.

During the time we owned the property, it was an average performer. From time to time, we had a few less-than-desirable tenants as well as vacancies. We also had a few stellar tenants such as the national mining company Asarco, who leased a bay and used it to store files and rock samples. For the most part, though, the small spaces attracted startups or other small companies that eventually outgrew their space, so we had a relatively normal rate of tenant turnover.

When the building was between six and seven years old, a tenant whose company leased two of the five bays approached us about buying the building. He needed more space and wanted to own rather than lease. We had to decide whether to take the opportunity to make a profit on our investment or to hold onto it and try to fill the space that this tenant would vacate.

We ended up selling the building to our tenant for $500,000. After paying off the balance of our mortgage, the proceeds we received at closing resulted in a 21% return per year on our original investment of $45,000! That was a good return for our efforts on a small development project in Spokane!

To generate that kind of a return, we bought the land for a bargain and completed the rezoning which increased its value. Then we managed the development and construction process efficiently. During our ownership we managed the property to maximize cash flow and then we used that cash flow to make extra principal payments on our mortgage. The result was a pretty handsome profit.

Done correctly, real estate development can be both personally and financially rewarding, but make sure you establish a solid base of real estate investment skills and the necessary financial resources that will maximize your chances for success.

It's tangible, it's solid, it's beautiful.
It's artistic, from my standpoint, and I
just love real estate.
                                    Donald Trump

~ 37 ~
Will Real Estate Appreciate Again?

Will real estate ever appreciate again? The answer is a resounding yes, and the factors that will contribute to long-term real estate appreciation are many.

Remember Will Rogers' quote about land? He said, *"Buy land. They ain't making any more of the stuff."* It's as true today as it was in his day. There is a finite amount of real property in the U.S., much of which is owned by the federal and state governments. Take out the properties that are geographically impossible to develop or that have no services such as water and sewer, and the resource of land becomes even more finite.

While we have a limited supply, we also have an inevitable increase in demand. Why is it inevitable? The population of the U.S. increases by roughly three million people each year, both through immigration and a positive birth-to-death ratio. The supply remains the same as the population continues to grow.

Now, add to the finite supply-inevitable demand dynamic one other element: growth management. Many cities and states are putting in place growth management regulations to slow urban sprawl and conserve natural resources. It's expensive to keep extending roads, water, sewer and other services farther out into areas of low-density development. Government entities are looking to curb such expansion.

The goal of growth management is to draw a boundary around an urban area and limit development on the rural side of that boundary. The corresponding goal is to stimulate infill development. Lawmakers want to encourage the creative use of underutilized property inside the urban circle and increase density, making use of the infrastructure that's already in place and reducing the future cost of expensive, new infrastructure.

Done properly, I believe growth management has many benefits to the environment and the economy. Some people will not agree with me, as additional government controls add to the cost of housing for everybody. However, as a nation we are heading in this direction, and we need to look for the opportunities it creates. As supply is constricted further by growth management and our population increases, prices will only go up.

Another factor on the supply side is that, while a number of historic commercial buildings are being preserved, many more old, obsolete buildings will be torn down to make way for new projects. About 350,000 homes nationwide are demolished each year.

Of course, some of this is theoretical. Supply does outweigh demand during down economic cycles, and we currently have a recession with an excess supply of homes that will limit new construction for a number of years. The market will balance out over time and when demand rises again, prices will also increase. Through typical, long-term real estate cycles, there will be solid and steady appreciation, especially in well-constructed, well-located, well occupied investment real estate. Well-located real estate has pretty consistently enjoyed solid long-term appreciation.

> *Don't wait to buy real estate,*
> *buy real estate and wait.*
> Will Rogers

~ Notes ~

~ 38 ~
Fun But Hard Work

I'm a mountain climber, and I see a lot of parallels between my favorite recreational activity and real estate investing. As in real estate, climbing mountains takes a lot of skill, training and effort. Also similarly, it involves a step-by-step process. People's motivational drive and physical abilities vary, and we come with different engines—some slow and some running at full speed at all times. But those differences aside, the step-by-step process is the same.

If you want to climb Mt. Rainier, for example, you set a date, hire a guide and train to get yourself in physical condition so you can endure the climb. You show up, and you take one step at a time until hopefully you reach the summit. Each climber heading up the mountain will climb at a different pace.

As with real estate, you will encounter challenges along the way. They will be mental, physical and emotional—and many times, the conditions will be out of your control.

A number of climbers will find the challenges too imposing and will turn around before they reach the top. You may not get to the top the first time you try, but if you are persistent you can eventually do it. Both climbing and real estate investing are a lot of hard work but in the end it is very satisfying to look back and see what you have accomplished. It is also great fun!

While real estate investing is a step-by-step process, it is different from many other goals in life we pursue. If you want to earn a particular college degree, the steps are somewhat defined for you. You go through a process and fulfill the specific requirements prescribed for you. Earning a college degree is hard work, but most people who put their minds to it and persevere will succeed.

I would contend that real estate investing is different. It's more abstract. There are more variables and unknowns outside of your control, and a vast amount of knowledge needs to be absorbed, understood, and applied to fluctuating conditions. Also, it takes a lot of self-confidence and the ability to take on the inevitable risk— again, similar attributes to climbing a mountain.

I remember going to a closing once with a group of dentists who were buying an office building. The way the deal was structured, each partner was personally liable for the whole loan amount, which was about $1.2 million. The bottom line was, if things went bad, the partner with the largest checkbook would be responsible for the entire amount. In the end, one of the dentist's spouses didn't want to sign the loan papers and assume that risk.

Compared to investing in the stock market, real estate investing is a lot more time consuming and complicated. If you want to buy a stock, you call your stockbroker or go online and buy it yourself. You need to do your homework, of course, but once you make up your mind, you just buy it. Real estate is much more time intensive.

There are a lot of get-rich-quick books that tell you real estate investing is easy. They tell you anyone can do it and make a lot of money. A lot of people do it and make money; in fact, more substantial wealth is created through real estate investments than any other type of investment. But the old adage is still true: "*If it was easy, everybody would be doing it.*" It takes hard work.

For people like me, hard work is a relative term when it comes to real estate investing. I revel in the challenge of it! It gives me a great sense of accomplishment when I negotiate the price of and buy a piece of property that I have worked hard to find. If you develop a passion for real estate investing, you too can learn the skills that are required to climb, one step at a time, to the top of your own real estate mountain.

Do the hard jobs first.
The easy jobs will take care of themselves.
Dale Carnegie

~ Notes ~

~ 39 ~
My Modus Operandi

Now that you have read about the real secrets of real estate investing, let's boil it down to the very simple nuts and bolts. In 1980 at the age of 25, I set a very simple goal to purchase one piece of property per year. Fortunately, I have been able to achieve that goal. I may have been a little green behind the ears back then, but I had some good mentors who pointed me in the right direction. Along the way, I refined my investing style and tried to learn from my mistakes. I was also lucky to partner with some more experienced real estate investors who taught me their investing secrets. Through time and experience, my *modus operandi* became the following.

My "formula" boils down to this: Purchase or build a high quality building in a favorable location with plenty of parking, and keep it leased to good tenants. Take good care of the property, making sure that it is well-maintained at all times. In other words, take a long-term approach to your real estate investing.

My goal, as well as my partners', is to hold our properties for the long haul, so keeping them in good condition is important to us. You would be amazed how many investors do not keep up their properties, but instead try to squeeze every dollar they can from their properties and spend it. You can't say to the wood stove, *"Give me some heat and I will give you some wood."* You must reinvest to keep your properties in good condition and attractive to your tenants.

Additionally, I specialized and focused most of my investing in office buildings. I have owned a wide variety of real estate over the years but my main area of expertise has been office buildings. As you specialize in one type of property, you learn all the unique characteristics of that property type, and you greatly increase your investing skills.

When we began to generate cash flow from our properties, we established a reserve for unexpected future expenses. The amount of the reserve varied depending on the property. With this reserve we always had cash in the bank in case we needed it. At that stage in life, my partners and I had enough income from our jobs to feed our families so we did not need the cash flow from our properties to live on. After the reserve was funded, we would use all future cash flows to make extra principal payments on our mortgages. These payments were in addition to our regular mortgage payments. With this plan we learned over time that we could pay off our mortgages in as little as thirteen years.

It is amazing how quickly time passes and all of a sudden your mortgages start paying off. My business partner Dave Black always says, "*There are no bad real estate investments as long as you live long enough.*" So time and real estate do work well together. As time goes on, the operation of your properties kind of goes on autopilot. Of course, each property is different. The interest rates on your mortgages will vary with each property you purchase. Your cash flow will vary from property to property. Some properties will have more vacancy over the course of your ownership. Other properties will stay full, producing consistent cash flow. If, when at all possible, you make extra principal payments on your mortgages, you will get those mortgages paid off sooner. You will be amazed at how quickly you can do it. Then of course, you will have achieved the goal of *Cash Flow Forever!*

As I mentioned earlier in this chapter, if you take the long-term approach to investing you must keep your properties in tiptop shape. There is no use in working hard for years to pay off your mortgages and end up with a bunch of junky, dilapidated buildings. The goal is to end up with paid-for buildings in top condition that will produce *Cash Flow Forever.*

Having a paid for-building gives you a lot of flexibility. With no mortgage, you can rent the property at whatever rent you need to attract a tenant. Other property owners with mortgages will be forced to try and get enough rent to cover their mortgage payments.

You can do what it takes to attract a tenant, especially in a slow market. If you need to make improvements for a new tenant, it is easy to borrow against a paid-for building since you will have the rent from the new tenant to make the payments on the improvement loan. You also have the option of selling the building and financing the sale yourself. You can consider whatever down payment you want and receive payments from the buyer on a mortgage for the balance you are owed.

When you are able to pay off the mortgage on your property it does not matter whether it is a single family rental home or a large commercial building. Those cash flow checks are a nice reward for all your hard work, and they do add up. The more paid-for properties you own, the more cash flows in the door.

So now that you know the real secrets to real estate investing, put this information into action!

An intelligent plan is the first step to success. The man who plans knows where he is going, knows what progress he is making and has a pretty good idea when he will arrive. If you don't know where you are going, how can you expect to get there?

Basil S. Walsh

~ 40 ~
Take Action!

Nike's old slogan refers to athletics, but the shoemaker also captured an essential element of real estate investing: *Just do it!*

Hopefully, you will be inspired when you finish this book. You now have some new knowledge that you can use to build wealth through real estate investing. What are you going to do? Are you going to put this book on a shelf and forget about it? Are you going to give it to a friend and tell them they should read it? Or are you going to do something to improve your financial future and the future of your family?

Unfortunately, it's likely that some of you will not take much if any action. You may poke around a bit and look at some real estate, but then you will settle back into life as usual. Over the years, most of us establish patterns and habits. We wear the same clothes, eat the same foods, and socialize with the same people, all while living in the same house and driving the same kind of car. We become comfortable with these life style patterns and habits.

My goal in writing this book is to motivate you to step out of your current habits and take action. Make some changes in your life! Break the mold! Push the envelope! Stretch yourself in a new way! Just follow some of the tried and true principles of real estate investing in this book. The steps down the path have been provided for you.

I know you can do it. Formulate a simple plan and get started. Examine your resources, and if you don't have the funds to begin investing, map out a plan to come up with a down payment for your first investment. Set a timetable and start working on it before you stall and get comfortable *not* doing it. Then get out there and begin looking at properties and making offers.

It's never too late. We all know people who have never finished college. By the time they are in their mid-30s, they say, "Oh, I'm too old now." They're wrong. It will take the same amount of time to finish college no matter what age you are. They're going to be "too old" whether they finish their degree or not. A lady in my church recently finished her degree. She's 72 years old. Investing is the same way: it is never too late to get started.

They say ordinary people accomplish extraordinary things because they try. Just try—and you will start down a path that will be new and rewarding, with opportunities you don't even know are out there.

I am just an average guy who grew up in a small town in Iowa. I was fortunate to find a couple of great mentors and read a few great books that put my life on a different track. You can do the same thing. *Just do it!*

Whatever you can do, or dream you can, begin it.
Boldness has genius, power and magic in it.
                    Johann Wolfgang von Goethe

Appendix A

Read All About It!

Think and Grow Rich by Napoleon Hill

How to Wake Up the Financial Genius Inside You by Mark Haroldsen

How I Turned $1,000 into $3 Million of Real Estate by Bill Nickerson

Winning Through Intimidation by Robert Ringer

How to Make $1 Million in Real Estate in Three Years Starting With No Cash by Tyler Hicks

Zeckendorf: An Autobiography of William Zeckendorf by William Zeckendorf

Trump: The Art of the Deal by Donald J. Trump and Tony Schwartz

How Real Estate Fortunes Are Made by George Bockl

Trammell Crow Master Builder: The Story of America's Largest Real Estate Empire by Robert Sobel

Nothing Down by Robert Allen

Exchanging Up by Gary Gorman

Appendix B

Real Estate Investing Terminology

Amortization: The process of paying off a real estate mortgage or note by making regular monthly payments of principal and interest over a set time frame.

Annual Debt Service: The total of your monthly mortgage payments for one year.

CAMS: Common Area Maintenance expenses. These expenses are usually billed to tenants based on the percentage of the property that they occupy as their space relates to the total square footage in the whole property. These expenses include but are not limited to landscaping, snow plowing, common area janitorial services, electricity for parking lot lights and signs, water, sewer, garbage services and other common expenses for maintaining the premises. These expenses are usually defined in the landlord's lease.

Capitalization (Cap) Rate: A capitalization rate, or cap rate, is a valuation tool used by bankers, appraisers and real estate investors to determine the value of a property. It is simply a relationship between the property's net operating income and the value of the property *(See Chapter 25, Cap Rates).*
Cash on Cash Return: The percentage return you will

receive based on dividing the amount of annual net cash flow from a property by the amount of down payment put down when you purchased the property. An example would be:

Annual net cash flow:	$10,000
Down payment invested at closing:	$200,000
Cash on cash return:	5%

Change Order: A document that spells out and keeps track of any change or changes to a construction contract or project, and the cost of the changes requested.

Common Area: The lobby, bathrooms and other common areas of a building. Common area square footage does not include vertical penetrations of the building which are defined as elevators, stair wells, ducts and chases.

Contingencies: Issues that must be satisfied by a purchaser during a set period of time before the purchaser elects to move forward with the closing of the purchase of the property.

Contingency Period: A period of time given by the seller of a property to a potential purchaser, to study all aspects of the property before the purchaser commits to finalize the purchase.

Contract Rent: The rent agreed to under the lease with a tenant

Debt Coverage Ratio: A factor used by lenders to

determine the maximum amount of annual mortgage payments they will allow based on a property's net operating income. It's used to provide the lender with a margin of safety when making a loan

Deficiency Judgment: A judgment obtained by a lender against a borrower who has been foreclosed upon. The lender sells the property that was pledged as security for the loan and if the sale proceeds do not cover the amount owed to the lender (including unpaid interest, costs and legal fees), the lender obtains a deficiency judgment for the amount of their loss against the borrower. Laws vary from state to state, and a deficiency judgment can only be obtained if the borrower has personally guaranteed the loan.

Due Diligence: The investigation and study of all aspects of the property that is performed by a purchaser during a contingency period.

Duplication: The act of duplicating, or making a copy of something. This is a key principal to successful real estate investing. Once you find a profitable formula for investing, duplicate your efforts and repeat the process.

Effective Gross Income: The income a building is generating after factoring in vacancy and credit loss.

Expenses: All of the expenses required to operate a building.

Gross Rent: When a tenant pays gross rent, the tenant

makes one rental payment to the landlord, and the landlord pays all of the building's operating expenses.

Load Factor: A percentage that is applied to the tenant's useable square footage to determine rentable square footage. For example, if the load factor is 15% and the tenant occupies 1,000 useable square feet, the tenant would pay rent on 115% of the space they occupy or 1,150 square feet of space. Essentially, the company would be paying for the space it uses plus 150 square feet of common area. Consequently, their share of the common area is *loaded* on to the tenant's useable square footage. Load factors vary depending upon how much common area is in a building. Load factors will also vary from market to market around the United States.

Market Rent: What a vacant space in a building should rent for in the market.

Modified Gross Rent: The tenant pays the rent plus a portion of the building's operating expenses. The expenses that the tenant is asked to pay can vary from landlord to landlord.

Negative Leverage: Borrowing at an interest rate that is greater than the cap rate.

Net Operating Income (NOI): The remaining income after operating expenses are subtracted from the effective gross income. The net operating income is an investor's cash flow if there is no mortgage on the property. If there is a mortgage, the net operating income goes toward the mortgage payment and any left-over money is the owner's cash flow.

Net Rent: When a tenant pays a net rent, the tenant usually pays all of the building's operating expenses or their prorate share of operating expenses if they are in a multi-tenant building in addition to their rent payment.

Net Rentable Area (NRA): The space on which the tenant is charged rent.

Non-recourse Financing: When the lender agrees to only take back the property as their recourse in case of default.

Positive Leverage: Borrowing at a rate that is less than the cap rate.

Potential Gross Income: The income a building can generate if it is fully leased.

Rentable Square Footage: The useable square feet occupied by the tenant plus the tenant's prorated share of the building's common area.

Tax-deferred Exchange: Allows a property owner to defer all or part of the capital-gains tax from the sale of one property by using the proceeds from its sale to acquire another in-kind investment property within a prescribed time frame.

Space Plan: The drawing done by a space planner or architect to show a prospective tenant how their business will fit into a space that the tenant is considering leasing.
Tenant Improvements (TIs): Upgrades that are needed or

requested by tenants leasing space from landlords. TIs can include but are not limited to newly sheet rocked and painted walls, floor covering, acoustical ceiling tiles and fluorescent lighting, plumbing, electrical, heating and air conditioning systems, and cabinetry. TIs can be paid for by the landlord, the tenants, or both.

Useable Square Footage: The square feet occupied by the tenant.

Vacancy Rate: The percentage of overall vacant square footage in a given group of buildings. For example, if there are 1 million square feet of Class A office space in a downtown core, and of that, 100,000 square feet are vacant, the downtown Class A vacancy rate is 10%. This is also referring to the percentage of vacancy in an individual building. Even if a building is 100% occupied, investors will typically apply a vacancy rate when doing a projection of the properties' long term income generating potential.

Appendix C

Additional Resources

Chapter 24 – The website for the Certified Commercial Investment Member Institute of the National Association of Realtors (CCIM) is www.ccim.com.

Chapter 32 – The following are websites where you can find samples of lease documents:
> www.legalcontracts.com
> www.rocketlawyer.com
> www.lawdepot.com

Chapter 35 – The following are websites where you can find helpful information on 1031 exchanges:

www.apiexchange.com – Asset Preservation, Inc., a subsidiary of Stewart Title Co.

www.orexco1031.com – Orexco 1031 Exchange, affiliated with Old Republic Life

www.ncs.firstam.com – First American Exchange Co., a First American Title Company

Bibliography

Think & Grow Rich, by Napoleon Hill, Random House
Publishing Group, Copyright 1960.

How to Wake up the Financial Genius Inside You by
Mark O. Haroldsen, Bantam, Doubleday, Dell Publishing
Group, 1980.

University of Success by Og Mandino, Bantam Books,
August, 1982.

About the Author

Jeff K. Johnson, CCIM SIOR, is the President of Black Commercial, Inc., the brokerage division of NAI Black. NAI Black is one of Spokane, Washington's largest property management and commercial real estate companies.

During his career, Jeff has specialized in the sale, leasing, and development of office buildings. Much of Jeff's work includes assisting Fortune 500 companies with the acquisition and disposition of corporate real estate. Jeff is also the managing general partner of numerous real estate investment partnerships. Church, community and industry affairs are an important focus of Jeff's life.

Jeff is married to his college sweetheart, Kae, and has three grown children and two grandsons.

A native of Forest City, Iowa, Jeff graduated from Forest City High School and attended Waldorf College.

Jeff is a hiker, rock and alpine climber.